Getting In to Grad School in Physics
(or other physical sciences)

Vincent Klug

Second Edition
Copyright 2014

Contents

Foreword

Some introductions are in order. My real name is not Vincent Klug, and I am not an author by trade. I'm a real grad student in a top-10 physics department. I'm publishing under an assumed name because I'd rather my students, colleagues, and employers think of me in terms of hopefully-forthcoming physics accomplishments, rather than as "that guy who wrote the grad school book." Still, I'd love your feedback on the book, and I'll try to answer any questions that you still have after reading: send me e-mails at VincentKlug100@gmail.com.

There are a million guides about how to get into college, or law school, or med school – but there exists almost nothing on how to get into graduate school for physics. This causes two problems: first, applicants rush through the application process, make poor decisions, and miss great opportunities. Applying to graduate school is a process that requires a *lot* of time and effort. Second, applicants have few resources for asking questions about the application process. This is so dire that students often resort to asking strangers on the internet via online "communities."

This book aims to remedy these problems. It has two goals:

- to synthesize much of the information on how physics graduate school works in the United States

- to walk you through your application to grad school, with answers and advice for common situations

I recommend using this book as early as possible. Most students order this book after senior year has already started – and that's okay, I have lots of advice for such students. But if possible, I recommend buying this book even earlier, as a sophomore or junior. Grad school admissions are based on what you did in college, and so it's best to learn the rules of the game as early as possible.

If you're applying for grad school in another science, this book will still be useful, as the application process is nearly identical.

Good luck on your application.

-"Vincent Klug"

Chapter 1

How Grad School Works

Definition: *Graduate School* is typically a 5-7 year process during which you will be paid a stipend while you take coursework and do original research in order to earn a PhD.[1]

1.1 Is Grad School for Me?

Let me start by dispelling a terrible rumor:

Rumor: It's impossible to get a science-related job with only a bachelor's degree in physics.

The truth is that there are lots of well-paying jobs that require a BS in physics (or any other physical science). In addition to knowing physics, you have three key skills that employers really want:

1. You know math. The financial sector, for example, needs to apply differential equations to a specific application (finance).

---

[1]There are lots of variations of this standard program (such as the master's degree); we'll get to those later.

It's much easier for financial firms to hire physicists and teach them economics than it is to hire economists and teach them differential equations!

2. You can analyze data objectively. Businesses have lots of pre-conceived notions about the way their businesses "should" be run, and they desperately need objective, emotionless data analysts like you to tell them how to improve their performance. This can really be a good deal: you'll get paid a very high salary for interesting work, and you get to move from company to company every few years.

3. You know computer programming (or can learn it quickly) and basic science. As a result, lots of engineering firms, consulting firms, IT firms, and so forth will hire you as a programmer, to write websites or make mathematical models for engineering applications.

These jobs tend to pay rather a lot and require real technical knowledge. They can offer quite a lot of freedom in terms of where and how you work. Better yet, they leave time (and money) for a life outside of work – a luxury you will most likely not be allowed in grad school. Despite these numerous perks, many grad school applicants don't even consider entering the private sector. This may be because of the second terrible rumor:

Rumor: If you don't know what to do after college, grad school is the logical step.

This rumor is particularly insidious: grad school is hard! It will consume 40-80 hours per week for 5-6 years, in exchange for which you'll get paid about the same as a fast food employee. Dividing your earnings by the number of hours worked, it's not unusual to get something like $3-4 per hour. Moreover, the payoff is pretty low: few of the jobs that require a PhD pay significantly higher than the private-sector jobs mentioned above. Worse yet, we have too many newly-minted PhDs in physics, and too few jobs that require one.

It may sound like I'm trying to talk you out of grad school. I'm really not, but I do want you to seriously ask yourself if grad school is the right choice. Here's why: most students don't.

The thought of taking on the challenges of grad school probably appeals to you. In addition, many of your friends are going to grad school, all of your professors went to grad school, and you've been in some school or another your whole life. It's therefore very easy to jump on the bandwagon, completely forgetting what grad school is for. Grad school is where research physicists are trained.[2] If you want to be a research physicist, then attending grad school is a logical and necessary step. Otherwise, you may want to carefully examine your motivations for applying.

Students often ask "Should I go to grad school?" (what they're really asking is "Should I choose a career as a research physicist?") That's a question only you can answer, but I will help by listing several traits that most successful grad students share:

---

[2]It may be useful to offer a formal definition of "research physicist." A research physicist is generally employed by a university, government laboratory, or private laboratory to do research into basic or applied physics. Physics professors at large universities are examples of (very successful) research physicists.

- They did well in college. There are cases where mediocre college students go on to do great things in grad school, but those are the exception, not the rule.

- They have varied interests. There's nothing wrong with having a narrow list of interests, but it's unusual for research physicists. Successful research physicists are generally have wide interests not only in physics and math, but also in other sciences, the arts, and the humanities.

- They love physics and/or problem solving. If you have any other motive (money, prestige, etc.) there are easier ways to achieve those goals.

- They are (somewhat) social. The nerd stereotype is not all that accurate. Modern research physicists need to be able to communicate and work in close cooperation with others.

- They like being busy and doing several things at once. A typical day in research is rarely linear: one must often juggle several projects at once.

Now no two research physicists are identical, so don't be too alarmed if you don't fit all of these characteristics. If you're sure that grad school is the right choice, then you should trust yourself more than me! Nonetheless, grad school is a huge undertaking, and you owe it to yourself to make an informed decision rather than ignoring the issue with a stupid declaration such as "Well, I don't know what to do next, guess I'll go to grad school."

1.2   From Matriculation to Degree

If you're still reading, either I didn't scare you away from grad school or you're still thinking it over. Either way, you should have an idea of what it will be like. In this section, I'll skip to the end and discuss exactly what the PhD program entails.

You arrive on campus in September for orientation. You'll go to a few workshops learning how to be a teaching assistant, attend a lecture with the department chair, get a copy of the graduate student handbook, and are assigned an office. You'll also be given keys to the building, and you'll be put in the system for payroll and health insurance. You'll choose a teaching or research assignment, and be briefed on your other responsibilities as a physics department employee. A few days later, term begins.

The first year is devoted to general physics classes – these are essentially undergraduate courses on steroids. These core classes are almost always the same: classical mechanics, statistical mechanics, quantum mechanics, and electricity & magnetism, sometimes with added courses such as mathematical methods or experimental methods. You'll spend hours and hours doing lengthy problem sets, often in groups with the other grad students. Finals can be in-class or take-home; take-home finals are often 48 sleepless hours. Despite the long hours, you'll find the material very interesting, and will be surprised at how quickly you can master such difficult concepts. If you pass the classes at the minimum level (often a B), you'll continue to second year.

During the second year, students take different coursework depending on what type of physics they want to study. The coursework is often a bit easier this year, but there is a new threat of a comprehensive qualifying exam. These vary *a lot* by school: sometimes they are absent altogether, while at other times there are both oral and written components administered over a week long period. If the qualifying exam exists, you will be required to pass at the requisite level (often 50% or 70%) after a certain number of attempts (usually 2 or 3) in order to proceed with your PhD.

During the third year, coursework and qualifying exams are either finishing or finished. Students find a research advisor and do research with him/her full time. At this point, students are typically eligible for master's degrees. Students who remain in the PhD program continue doing research until they have enough to publish: this generally takes until the fifth year, but it can take much longer. After the fifth year, the department will start pressuring you to graduate. This pressure can be very severe, such as cutting off your funding, if enough time elapses. Some programs are more understanding than others.

During the final year, you will publish your results (hopefully) and also write your results into a dissertation. After your convince your advisor to approve the dissertation, you defend your results in front of a panel of judges, and an audience (other students and your family). Almost everyone who makes it this far eventually defends successfully. Finally, you submit a written copy of your dissertation to the graduate school. A few weeks later, you get a "congratulations" letter, instructions for ordering caps and gowns, and a diploma.

1.3   Degrees: MS vs PhD

You might be confused because up to now, we've been talking only about the PhD. What about the master's degree?

Indeed, graduate school in physics means you're working on one of two things: a Master's Degree (MS), or the confusingly-named "Doctorate of Philosophy" (PhD). As you might expect, the PhD program is longer and more rigorous than the master's program. In fact, PhD students usually qualify for a master's degree halfway through the PhD program.

So which program should you sign up for? For some graduate students this can be a big decision, but physics graduate students almost always go for the PhD. Students generally only obtain a master's degree in physics for one of the following reasons:

- They're in a PhD program but leave the program before graduating. If they complete a given amount of work before leaving (generally on the order of two years), they're given the MS as a "consolation prize."

- They graduate college and get a job in a technical field. After several years of work, the employer tells you that you need a master's degree before you can get promoted (this is nice because the employer generally pays the bills).

If you're reading this book, you're probably interested in the PhD. In fact, many reputable graduate schools do not offer a terminal master's degree.[3] Even if the MS degree is offered, the PhD program has another key advantage – money. MS programs generally require the student to pay the university; PhD programs generally have the opposite arrangement.

This book is written mostly for the benefit of those interested in the PhD (since that's more common), but will still be useful for those interested in the MS. Allow me a brief digression to discuss those aspects of graduate school specific to MS students.

For MS Students

One option available to you is to enter a PhD program, and then leave after you've done enough work to earn a master's degree (generally the first 2-3 years of the PhD program). The main advantage to this, of course, is money: the program will pay you to attend rather than billing you for tuition.

Let me be clear: it is highly dishonest and unethical to deceive the program about your plans. If you do so, you risk being thrown out of the program without any degree, or with poor letters of recommendation. Nonetheless, there's nothing to stop you from telling the program up-front that you will leave after achieving the master's degree. In fact, it is a good idea to e-mail before applying – use a brief paragraph to describe your qualifications and the reason you need an MS, and ask if they will be able to accommodate you.

---

[3]A "terminal master's program" is a program where students are expected to graduate after earning the master's degree. As discussed above, some students who intend to graduate with a PhD but fail to complete the program are awarded a master's degree as a consolation prize. These two types of master's degrees are fully equivalent and indistinguishable.

If you end up in a terminal master's program, most of this book is still relevant, especially the parts about the application process. However, there are some key differences from the PhD; let me spell those out here:

- Timeline. Master's programs generally take 2.5 years, but they can be as short as 1 year or as long as 4.

- Funding. Funded master's programs are very rare (though they do exist). In general, you will be expected to pay the program, either from your employer, an external fellowship (more on that later), or student loans. Student loans in physics can be very hard to find, so you'll want to begin that search concurrently with your applications.

- Program Description. Master's Degrees come in two "flavors" (it's not unusual for both flavors to be offered at a given school). The first option is that you graduate after completing the same coursework as the PhD students. This is certainly the flavor you'll get if you enter a PhD program and then leave early. The alternative is that you will do less coursework than the PhD students, but in addition you'll do research culminating in a short paper called a master's thesis. These two "flavors" result in equivalent and indistinguishable master's degrees – speak to your employer (if applicable) about which option is preferred.

- Location. PhD students often travel across the US (or from further away) to complete their PhD; master's students often remain local.

1.4   Finances

Now for some good news: reputable PhD programs generally pay you. In fact, you get the whole package: a stipend, tuition waiver, health insurance, and office space. Some PhD programs even offer discretionary funding, travel funds, and other perks.

How much do you get? I would estimate that most schools have a base salary of around $21,000 per year. But, this number is a function of at least three variables:

- The program's prestige. Top-10 programs generally pay less, on the (correct) assumption that most students will attend despite the low pay. Conversely, the least reputable programs tend to have more erratic pay schedules – some don't pay at all (more on that later), while others have lavish compensation packages hoping to deter grad students from attending more prestigious schools.

- Location. Expensive locations (such as Boston and coastal California) tend to pay better than cheap locations (such as the Midwest).

- You. Different students do not all get the same salary. Well-qualified students get higher offers; these offers can occasionally be further increased by negotiation (see section 5.2 for more about negotiation).

This last bullet point may seem particularly surprising, so let me explain where your funding comes from. You earn your salary in one of three ways:

page 17   1.4. FINANCES

- TAship. Graduate students assist with the teaching of undergraduate classes (this arrangement is called a "teaching assistantship" or TAship). Practically speaking, this means teaching a discussion section or laboratory section, grading homework or lab reports, and holding office hours. This generally involves 15-25 hours of work per week. Entering students often teach until they join a research group, at which point they are paid with an RAship.

- RAship. Graduate students work with a professor conducting original physics research (this arrangement is called a "research assistantship" or RAship). After joining a research group, students usually work with a group as an RA until graduation.

- Fellowship. Well-qualified students may be offered a fellowship. This generally means receiving a paycheck without the necessity of teaching or doing research. Students often take advantage of this in order to take extra coursework, or to do research "for free" with the advisor of their choice (the advantage being that the advisor does not have to use his/her own funds to pay the student).

These three classes of employment usually have different pay rates. In addition, unique combinations such as a "partial fellowship" are common.

Another important factor to consider is how your tuition is paid. Some schools waive your tuition altogether, others pay your tuition in addition to your salary, and then bill you for the tuition. This subtle difference is important for tax reasons: in the latter case, your tuition is taxable income.

Here's another common question involving the money: what if I get admitted to a grad school, but the program doesn't offer any money?

In general,[4] such offers should be rejected. Either the program is broke, or else they're so underwhelmed by your application that they're not willing to pay you. Either way, not a good sign! Beyond that, the PhD does not guarantee you a high-paying job. Graduating with an advanced degree, no job, and lots of debt really is the worst case scenario.

So far we've only discussed getting paid by the school that admitted you. Wouldn't it be nice if you could get funding from some other source? This would solve a lot of problems: grad school is competitive because they have many more qualified applicants than they are able to afford. If you are able to convince an external agency to pay for your grad school (to give you an *external fellowship*), then it will be much easier to be admitted.

Perhaps the most well-known of the external fellowships is the NSF Fellowship, which provides for full tuition in addition to a stipend. Other fellowships are funded by the Department of Energy, Department of Defense, or local agencies, which vary by school. These

---

[4]and I really do mean "in general"; there are lots of perfectly valid reasons why you should accept such an offer. For example, non-funded master's degrees are the norm.

fellowships tend to have extended application processes (as or more difficult than the grad school applications themselves) but are definitely worth the effort. In addition to increasing your odds of being admitted to grad school, they will also eliminate the need for you to teach during your first few years. Better yet, you will often be able to select the research advisor of your choice: research advisors are quite happy to "hire" grad students that don't need to be paid!

1.5   Admissions

You should be aware that admission to graduate schools is a *very* competitive process. Top-10 programs typically have acceptance rates below 10%. Large, reputable universities typically have acceptance rates well below 25%. Moreover, most people applying to graduate school are smart, qualified physics students. These are very low acceptance rates. "Terrified" is an appropriate response!

The other thing you should know right from the beginning is that *admissions* is really a misnomer. What's actually going on is that graduate students are being *hired*. What's the difference? *Admissions* suggests an implied expectation of fairness: students who meet a given standard deserve to be admitted, the rest do not. But the physics department is hiring graduate students, and it will do so at the convenience of the department. It doesn't matter who is most qualified, who has the best grades, or the most research experience. The only thing that matters is which students meet the *department's* needs for that year. As a result, it can be very difficult to predict how your application will be received.

Now for some good news (for domestic students at least): citizenship, gender, and race are very important criteria to almost all physics departments. To this end, all domestic students (that is, US citizens, permanent residents, or someone who holds refugee, asylee, or Jay Treaty status) have a big advantage. Females and members of underrepresented minorities (African-Americans, Hispanic-Americans, Native Americans, etc.) are given an even larger advantage.[5]

Many graduate schools will directly give members of these groups preference during applications; nearly all will be more flexible on salary and other perks in order to attract such graduate students. Hence, the very low acceptance rates are actually considerably higher for domestic students (and higher still for members of underrepresented minorities); unfortunately they are lower still for international students – particularly those from overrepresented areas (most notably, Eastern Asia).

Despite these generalities, all applications are considered individually, and you have some chance of being admitted regardless of which category you fall into. Much of this book will discuss how you can work this system to your advantage.

---

[5]This may seem like unproven speculation, but it is actually well-established. Underrepresented minorities are *highly* underrepresented in physics, and programs are quite proud of taking extra steps to remedy this.

1.6   Everything Else

That's almost everything I can tell you about grad school itself in a systematic fashion. The next few chapters are devoted to the application process - but first I will answer other common questions and concerns about graduate school in question and answer format.

I have really bad grades / low test scores / no research experience.   Do I have any chance of getting into grad school?

Yes! It's almost always possible to get into a PhD program[6], but it will obviously be more challenging. You'll want to choose the programs you apply to carefully: you (obviously) have a better chance of being admitted at a less competitive university. You may not be able to get a funded offer, so you'll want to think carefully about whether you're willing to pay for graduate school.

Let me be more specific. If you meet the following guidelines, it's likely that there is a program out there willing to fund you as you earn your PhD:

1. You have/will have a bachelor's degree in science or math from a recognized college or university.

2. You have at least a 2.5 QPA.

3. There's something interesting or unusual about your application. This could be high test scores, solid research experience,

---

[6]The physics PhD is different than some other advanced degrees in this regard. In medicine, for example, it doesn't matter where you go, but it's very dificult to get in anywhere. Physics is exactly the opposite.

a glowing letter of recommendation, a unique life story, solid work experience, etc.

If you meet these minimum criteria, you should at least apply for graduate school admission. Even so, I suggest that you focus on less competitive programs, and have a backup plan as well. It's also a good idea to e-mail the programs you're considering with a *brief* paragraph discussing your qualifications and asking if your application is likely to be competitive.

If you do not meet these criteria, I suggest you take another year as an undergraduate so that you can improve your grades, retake your tests, and gain some research experience.

Will it affect my application if I postpone graduate school for a year, and take another year as an undergraduate?
A small handful of programs penalize those students who take a fifth year as an undergraduate (most of these programs are hyper-competitive to begin with). So if you have some top-notch schools in mind, you may wish to e-mail them and ask whether they have a preference.

In general, though, taking a fifth year is fine, so long as you have a proportional number of extra accomplishments. If it took you five years just to get through the physics major, then that's less impressive. If you used the extra year productively (to take extra coursework or gain extra research experience, for example), then it is likely to help your application. As discussed in the previous question, an extra year can really strengthen a weak application.

Am I too old to go to grad school? Will I be given a hard time because of being female or a minority?

No! Older students are often successful. The bigger concern is that physics knowledge is forgotten fairly quickly; you'll want to submit recent test scores to show the admissions committee that you still remember the prerequisite knowledge for the program.

As for members of minority groups, departments generally have zero tolerance for hazing and discriminatory behavior. On the contrary, departments are very eager to have you, and are willing to take significant steps to make sure that the environment is productive and welcoming.

I don't have a physics degree. Can I still apply to physics graduate school?

Yes, but the admissions committee will be concerned about your background knowledge. It is a good idea to take as many upper-division physics classes as possible. You might be able to get away with skipping some of the labs, but it's essential that you take all the lecture courses, even the upper-level ones like statistical mechanics. You'll also want to take (and study for) the Physics GRE.

What advice do you have for someone who is looking to go back to graduate school after a career in something else?

First, make sure you have the background knowledge. The best thing to do take undergraduate courses in physics and math at a local university. Some students prefer to self-study and then use exam scores to show that they know the material – this can work, but it's better to actually take the classes and get good grades.[7] Either way, you need to actually be able to solve problems – vague memories or concepts won't be enough.

Second, you'll have to fill out an application like anyone else. Make sure your test scores are recent, even if you have to retake the tests. The difficulty will be the letters of recommendation. If you took classes (recently) at a college, the professors there can write for you. If you self-studied, then the letters will be a real problem. There's not much I can say in this situation, though I will say it's better to have a great letter from a non-physicist than a crappy letter from a physicist.

Don't worry too much about your (lack) of research experience – programs understand the challenges associated with being a second-career student. Certainly any classes or research experiences you can get will help a lot, but you shouldn't let your lack of research experience prevent you from applying.

Apply a lot of places. Due to the small statistics, schools tend to be a bit less logical about these applications, so you might get some suprises (good or bad).

Finally, timetables. Many people have vague ideas that they will one day get a physics PhD, and yet each year, there are very few

---

[7]Many students try to avoid taking classes because they feel awkward being in a room full of 20-year-old college students. This is understandable, but it's something you'll likely have to get over at some point.

second-career graduates. So perhaps the single biggest piece of advice I can offer is to be impatient: either set a detailed, ambitious timetable with a specific year in which you will start grad school, or choose a more achievable goal.

I want to focus on something multidisciplinary. Is physics graduate school an appropriate way to do this?

Yes, but you'll want to choose your program carefully. Many programs are specifically designed for a particular interdisciplinary study.

Can I take a gap year before starting grad school?

Yes. There are two options here: you can apply now and defer, or you can apply during your gap year. Deferring is generally the better option, *but* it's only possible at some grad schools. Most students who defer end up applying during the gap year. This can help or hurt your application: if you're doing something useful (traveling, doing physics, etc.) and can demonstrate that your physics skills are not atrophying (such as by retaking the exams), then it will likely help your application.

I need a long break. Is it possible that I can take more than one year off and then come back for the PhD?

It's possible; in fact, some recommend it. I don't. Many students plan to go back for the PhD, but few do. This may be because:

- After making real money and incurring real responsibilities, you won't want to or be able to go back to the grad student salary.

- The long hours of work are something you've been getting accustomed to over the past 4+ years; they will seem very difficult when you return to school after a long break

- Physics knowledge is forgotten very quickly

- Grad school is in some sense an apprenticeship; many older students are reluctant to be an apprentice to someone of the same age

That said, many students do overcome the odds and return to work on their PhD. The application process for these students is the same as for any other students, though it's especially important to retake those exams. Exam scores are good for five years, but most programs will assume that you've forgotten most of your physics knowledge unless you retake the exams and do well on them. You'll also want to think carefully about your letters of recommendation: you may want to ask for some of them before leaving college.

My wife/husband/boyfriend/girlfriend is also applying to grad school. Is it possible that we'll both get into the same program?

It's possible, but this is a tricky situation. If your partner's program is also very competitive (especially if he/she is also in physics), then it's quite unlikely that both of you will be admitted to your top-choice program. You'll therefore want to think carefully about the relative importance of your relationship and your graduate application. When you proceed with applications, I don't suggest mentioning your relationship until one of you is admitted. See section 5.3 for more information about this.

How many students fail out of grad school? What are my options if I do so?

In general, 50-60% of those students who enter a PhD program leave with a PhD within 10 years. About 30% of those who leave the program leave of their own volition: they prefer to transfer to another school, or they decide they don't want to do physics anymore, or they have a personal situation that causes them to resign. Simple subtraction would suggest, then, that 10-20% of students fail out of the program, either by failing qualifying exams, or failing courses, or not finding an advisor, or not obtaining publishable results.

As usual, the whole story is more complicated. These numbers vary *a lot* by school. Some programs deliberately hire many more grad students than needed, so that they can be used as teaching assistants. Others try very hard not to fail anyone out. Still others don't fail people out, but the working environment is such that an abnormally high percentage of students transfer or quit. These numbers also vary from research group to research group! As a result of all these fluctuations, it's a very good idea to ask for an "overall yield" before accepting an offer of admission.

If you do fail out, your options are to transfer to another grad school (this normally requires a big jump downwards in terms of prestige) or to start looking for a job. Either way, you should try to get a master's degree before leaving the program.

Is it easier to get in some years than others?

Yes. Every school fluctuates from year to year, but across the board, it is harder to be admitted when the economy is bad. A bad economy will cause state support of universities to decrease, which results in less spots. Further, less jobs will be available, so more will apply to grad school "as a last resort."[8]

I'm a foreign student. How is the process different for me?

Once grad school starts, the process is exactly the same, with lots of extra bureaucracy. One key difference is red tape involving funding: most schools will have opportunities for grad students to earn extra money, but foreign students do not necessarily qualify for these.[9] Same with fellowships – most fellowships are only for domestic students. Also there's lots of paperwork to keep Immigration happy– but your school will walk you through that. If you apply for citizenship – and students often do – there's a lot of red tape there as well.

There are more significant differences during the application process. In general, you're at a disadvantage – remember that students are admitted at the convenience of the department, and departments are generally under a lot of pressure to have mostly domestic students. Worse yet, there are many qualified international students and few spots available. But let me be more specific by breaking this down by situation.

---

[8]However, most jobs in physics are inelastic with respect to the economy – if getting a job sounds preferable to going to grad school, you should definitely apply for a job regardless of the economy.

[9]On the other hand, your home country might offer external fellowships for grad students studying abroad – these are well worth investigating

- If you did your undergraduate in the US and became a US citizen, then you are a domestic student and the process will be exactly the same as any other domestic student – though you'll be subject to affirmative action, like all other domestic students.[10]

- If you did your undergraduate in the US but are not a US citizen, then your application should look very similar to domestic undergraduate students. However, you'll still (in many programs) be competing against other international students, and it will therefore be more difficult to be admitted.

- If you're coming from a developed country similar to the US (like Canada or Western Europe) then the process is exactly the same, just a little harder, since admissions committtees are under pressure to admit domestic students.

- If you're coming from what is perceived to be an underdeveloped country (like many of the African countries), then you'll have a huge advantage in your application: physics departments love diversity and students who "overcame the odds."

- If you're coming from India, China, or Japan, then your application will be significantly different. For one thing, you'll not be expected to have much research experience, but you will be expected to have nearly perfect grades. For that reason, many students take an entire year off in order to study for exams. For another thing, there are many qualified students

---

[10]If you're not familiar with this idea, this refers to a paradigm under which schools directly give preference to members of underrepresented groups, especially racial minorities.

from those three countries, but very few spots for them in American universities – so admissions rates for these students are almost always in the single digits, even at less competitive programs. You'll therefore want to apply to a lot of schools, including less competitive ones.

No matter where you're from, you'll need to know the language – be sure to take the TOEFL (Test of English as a Foreign Language) and do well on it – but that's not really good enough, to be successful you'll need a superb knowledge of the language. Most schools have minimum TOEFL scores which are quite high.

The other disadvantage you'll have as a foreign student is directly after admission. Once an offer is made, the admissions committee's job is to convince domestic students to accept their offer of admission. Most foreign students will not be "wooed" in this manner – if you decline, there are plenty of other qualified foreign students to take your spot.

How important are external fellowships? How hard are they to get?

This varies by external fellowship. In general, you have the best chance of getting an external fellowship if you're very active outside of physics: for example, if you have lots of multidisciplinary or volunteer experience. In that case, it's a very good idea to get an external fellowship to pay the bills and ask the department only for admission (especially since the department may be significantly less impressed by these "unrelated" accomplishments). On the other hand, if all your activities are physics related, you'll have a better chance of being funded by the department. Some external fellow-ships are funded by industry; these would be a very good idea if you hope to eventually work for industry.

Should I go to graduate school abroad?

Not unless you get into one of the very best foreign programs, such as Oxford, Cambridge, or the Max Planck Institute. In general, the US has the best graduate schools: if you want to stay in the US, you'll definitely want a US degree; if you want to eventually work abroad, you'll be particularly desirable if you attended an American graduate school. The reason it's so difficult to be an international applicant is because American graduate schools are the best in the world; domestic students would, in general, be poorly advised to trade away that advantage.

I went to a really small school. Will I be able to get into grad school?

Yes, but you will face some additional challenges. For one thing, research experience will be much harder to get. For another, it will be difficult to evaluate your coursework, so good grades and high test scores are particularly necessary. Also, small physics depart-ments often don't have advanced classes, so you may have to take extension courses in another university. If it's early enough, you may want to consider transferring to a larger school.

For whatever reason, I'm thinking of applying to two dif-ferent grad programs (such as applying to English or chem-istry in addition to physics, for example) and seeing what

happens. Good idea?

There are lots of good reasons not to. These include:

- Applying to two programs suggests that you aren't really committed to either. You should examine your motivations carefully.

- Doing two full-scale application processes will be twice as expensive and twice as time consuming.

- Doing anything less than two full-scale application processes increases the odds that you'll miss a great opportunity.

- Unless you have separate recommenders for each program, your recommenders will have to write double the number of letters, which they may complain about.

- Physics requires two standardized tests (more on those later); your other application will likely require at least one more. As your study time becomes more divided, your exam scores become lower.

- Some universities only accept one application per person per year, so you might not be able to apply to both programs at a particular school.

Many people would claim these drawbacks are fundamentally insurmountable. For the most part, I agree – but if the particulars of your situation allow you to avoid these drawbacks, then I encourage you to proceed with your dual application.

For whatever reason, I'm thinking of working a job during grad school. Is that possible?

Some programs allow this; others don't. Personally, I feel that working an off-campus job, unrelated to physics, is unethical (not to mention exhausting). Your program is paying for all of your expenses so that you can spend as much time as possible contributing to physics by learning, teaching, and doing research. That said, some schools do allow this; you can send an e-mail to programs you're considering if this is important to you.

I'm still in high school, but I want to eventually do a physics PhD. Where should I go to college?

There are many things to consider, so I suggest looking at one of the "choosing a college" books (of which there are many) for a comprehensive answer. In terms of your eventual application to graduate school, there are really only two things you need to know:

1. Things will be much harder at a small school, as discussed before. I suggest going somewhere with (a) a recognized physics department, that (b) offers advanced classes in physics, and (c) gives undergraduates the opportunity to conduct original research. There are several hundred schools that meet these criteria.

2. It is true that your application will be given an advantage if you attend a *very* prestigious undergraduate school. Don't overstate this advantage. If you get into and can afford to attend a famous, prestigious school, then that's great – but if not, you'll still have every chance to get into a great graduate school.

Chapter 2

Strengthening Your Application

Now that you've decided (tentatively or otherwise) to apply to grad school, it's time to do whatever you can to strengthen your application. Your applications will have many components, but they really come down to two things: how much physics you know, and how much research you've done. The former will be measured by grades and tests; the latter will be measured by a CV and letters of recommendation.

This chapter is designed for those students who still have time to make improvements, which will give you more to work with when the application process starts. If you're not yet a senior, this is the chapter you'll want to focus on. It gives advice related to coursework, studying for exams, and getting research experience. If your last year has already started, then you should skim this section, but read chapter four most carefully.

2.1   Grades

Time for another nasty rumor:

Rumor: College grades don't matter at all.

This one actually has a glimmer of truth: a large handful of the less competitive programs do ignore grades, focusing almost exclusively on research experience and letters of recommendation. But most programs consider grades as one of the most important components of your application. You'll spend your first two years as a grad student taking classes; no one wants you to start graduate school only to flunk out six months later.

Let me explain how your grades will normally be evaluated:

1. Any graduate coursework you've done will be carefully scrutinized. You are not expected to have completed any graduate coursework (and most applicants don't, even at the best schools). Still, if you have a passing grade in a grad physics class by the time your application is reviewed, that's a great way to reassure the committee that you'll be able to handle the coursework. If you're thinking of taking a graduate course during your fall semester, I suggest quantum mechanics (that's normally the most accessible course, assuming you've taken undergrad quantum).

2. Your core, upper-division physics courses grades will be examined thoroughly. These courses include classical mechanics, statistical mechanics, quantum mechanics, and electricity & magnetism. Advanced courses in circuit analysis, computa-

tional methods, mathematical methods, particle physics, and solid state physics will also count if you have them.

3. Other physics, math, chemistry, and computer science courses will be reviewed. Specific grades are less important here, but general trends will be observed, and anomalies will be noted.

4. Your general education requirements will be considered in a superficial manner. The only non-science classes that will be given significant weight are those that address the committee's concerns about you; for example, your English grades will be examined if your writing skills seem poor.

Majors & Minors

If it's still quite early in your college career, you may be wondering what you should choose as a major. This is an easy question: you should major in physics and take as many advanced physics courses as possible (while maintaining a very high QPA). In particular, you absolutely should take a course titled "quantum mechanics" (you probably took a course called "modern physics" that covered some quantum mechanics – that won't be enough). Other advanced courses will make your application more competitive and your time in grad school easier.

Students frequently pick up a minor or double major in math, or sometimes in chemistry, astronomy, geology, or even biology. These are less important than your advanced physics classes, but are still very helpful to your application. Math will be useful regardless of your research interests; the other sciences can be very helpful depending on what type of physics you choose to study.

Occasionally, students do a double major or a minor in something totally unrelated, such as English or theater arts. This is a very good idea if your application is otherwise excellent – grad schools love talented individuals with diverse interests. If your physics background is anything less than ideal, though, these majors/minors are probably not worth the effort.[1] They will distract you from learning physics and might cause the admissions committee to question either your commitment or your judgment.

Grades vs. Test Scores

Perhaps you're wondering whether grades or test scores hold more weight. If you went to a large or prestigious university with a recognized physics department, your grades will be much more important than your exam scores. If you went to a small school with a tiny physics department, your grades will carry less weight (more specifically, it will be very troubling if your grades aren't good, but no one will be impressed if your grades are good – they'll just look at your exam scores).

2.2   General GRE

The General GRE is a necessity for almost all grad schools, so you'll definitely want to take this exam. The good news is that you can take it very early: the first few weeks of senior year are ideal. That

---

[1] Of course, this answer is just from the perspective of grad school admissions. One would be rather pathetic if (s)he made every single decision in life based on pleasing the graduate school admissions committee!

way, you can finish this part of your application before your deadline crunch. Further, you'll be able to retest if necessary. Be aware that this exam is expensive: it costs almost $200 per attempt (and reporting your score to the places you apply can be even more expensive).

The General GRE has three components: verbal, writing, and math. These are exactly analogous to the SAT, only the verbal is harder and the math is easier. Although this exam is an absolute requirement for virtually all grad school applications, the scores are not as important as you might think. By virtue of being a physics major, you'll do great on the math, you'll do horribly on the verbal, and the writing will (hopefully) be decent. For most students, only this last section requires extensive preparation. Let's go through the pesky details, then we can examine each section individually.

Administrative Details

- This test is done on the computer in the United States; in some areas of the world a paper test is offered instead.

- Scores use the range 130-170, in one point increments. The writing section is scored between 0 and 6, in half point increments.

- The test is almost four hours long.

- You may cancel your scores before submitting the test; after your test is submitted, scores cannot be canceled. If you do not cancel your scores, the computer version will give you your verbal and math scores before you leave the testing facility. If you do cancel them, neither you nor the grad school will ever know what those scores were.

- You get four free score reports with each exam, additional score reports are $27 each (as of 2014). These additional score reports will have both your general and Physics GRE scores, so don't order them until both scores are available.

- The essays in the writing section can be sent to the grad school if the graduate school so requests.

- Sign up for this test online (www.ets.org/GRE); that website will provide you several options for when and where to take the computer version (less options for the paper version).

- You take all three sections on the same day; you cannot mix and match your test scores.

- If you take the GRE more than once, you may specify which sections to send to the grad school. If you send more than one set of scores, most grad schools will consider only the most recent score, but that varies by program.

Math section

These math section drills you on middle school math and basic reasoning skills. As a result, you really need a perfect or nearly perfect score to avoid raising any alarms. Scores in the range of 167-170 are considered perfect (every year, students get the stupid idea that they're going to be rejected because they got a 169. That's not even close to true). Lower scores, especially those below 160, are very alarming indeed: regardless of the circumstances, it does not bode well if you are flummoxed by middle school math problems!

The computer interface is pretty good: you're allowed to go back and change your answers, mark questions to return to later, and it even provides an on-screen calculator. Better yet, the *groups* of questions are adaptive but the questions are not – so you'll do your first set of pre-written math questions (and be allowed to preview them all), but your second set of math questions will be either hard or easy depending on how you did on the first set.[2]

All questions within a given section are given equal weight.

Verbal Section

Here's how admission committees discuss the verbal section:

1. Your verbal score is glanced at.

2. If your score is very low (usually below ~145, though this does vary) your application is moved to the "probably reject" pile.

3. Otherwise, you get a "check mark" and your score is never considered again.

The verbal section is really quite hard: all students are expected to have learned English while in college (but it's apparently OK that most students know less math after graduation than they knew originally). Further, this is the same test that English grad school applicants take. Only 10% of test takers (of *any* major) score above

---

[2]One of the GRE sections is experimental, and not used to calculate scores, so don't be alarmed if your second set seems really easy – it might just be the experimental set.

162, so don't be alarmed if you do poorly in this section.

As you can see in the algorithm above, your verbal score carries very little weight with the committee unless it's terribly low. If it is, you are likely to be rejected, *unless* there's something in your application to convince them that you really do have good grasp of the English language. This could be a high writing score, a well-written statement of purpose, a letter of recommendation from an English professor, or (for foreign students) a high TOEFL score.

Now it is true that a few programs will give you some credit for a stupendously high verbal GRE score. Programs do like diversity and well-roundedness. Even so, I don't suggest spending much time studying for this section, since it requires a *lot* of tedious hours in order to effect even a modest improvement to your score. Take a practice test under real test conditions and see how you do: unless your score is very low, there's no reason to study beyond that. If your score does need improvement, you are in for a tedious and time-consuming endeavor, one that will require a book specifically written for that purpose. But don't spend too much time trying to get a super-high verbal score; this is not an efficient use of your time.

Writing Section

The admissions committee will give you another perfunctory check mark on your application, but this one is perhaps a bit more important than the verbal. High writing scores are good news – physicists need to be able to communicate in order to be effective. While a high (5 or above) writing score will not get you in, it may help to turn things in your favor in a particularly close competition. As before, a very low score (below 3) can move you to the "probably reject" pile unless there's some evidence that you really do know how to write.

For this section, you are required to write two essays: in one you will be required to comment on a particular issue; on the other, you will be required to write a critique of an argument submitted to you. These essays will be typed in a computer application designed specifically for this test. It is a little clunky to use and it does not include a spell checker.

As for studying, I suggest that you read through a few sample essays before test day, and understand exactly what they're looking for. If you're *a little* worried about this section, you may wish to write your statement of purpose before taking the GRE, since the techniques used in the statement of purpose are highly useful on the GRE. If you're *very* worried about this section, you may wish to get a book specifically devoted to this section of the exam.

2.3   Physics GRE

This may be the first time you realized that the Physics GRE even exists, so let me give some background. The Physics GRE (PGRE) is a 170-minute, 100-question exam that tests your understanding of undergraduate physics.[3] It is required for nearly all graduate

---

[3]There are actually 7 subject exams offered; the other sciences are: biology, chemistry, mathematics, psychology, and "biochemistry, cell & molecular biol-

school admissions. It is offered only three times a year in the US: October (your best bet), November, and April. Your raw score is the number of questions right minus a guessing penalty. This score is then converted to a scaled score between 390 and 990.

This test is perhaps the first big difference between domestic and foreign students. Foreign students, especially those who did their undergraduate studies in Asia[4]– are expected to do very well on this exam (scores in the 900s are not at all unusual, near perfect scores are pretty much expected for competitive programs). Students who did their undergraduate studies in the US are allowed much lower scores: 800 is just about the top score that can be reasonably expected from a domestic student, even at the best programs.[5] If you went to a top undergraduate program and got good grades, then this part of your application is less important – low scores will be written off as a fluke. For everyone else, this test is crucial – it's the chance to redeem yourself if your grades aren't perfect, or to get them to take your application seriously if you went to a small school.

Applicants love to criticize this test because it involves a lot of memorization and less critical reasoning. It is true that many questions require only a superficial understanding of the topic being tested.

---

ogy." If you're applying to one of those programs, you'll probably have to take the corresponding test.

[4]I say Asia because undergraduates in Europe or elsewhere generally have undergraduate programs very similar to those in the US. There are also fewer applicants from other continents than from Asia.

[5]Sound unfair? Only a little. The trade off is that Asian students are generally held to a much lower standard with respect to research experience (since research experiences are much scarcer in Asia). Further, it is common for Asian students to take an entire year off to study for exams.

Still, this test is able to measure both the amount of physics you've seen before and how much "walking around" physics you know. Both are actually important quantities to measure.

As for studying, I have no magic formula. Here's a good general algorithm for you:

First Step. Take a quick look over a practice exam, so you have a vague idea of what level the questions are at.

Second Step. Get an intro to physics book (I make a recommendation in sec. 7.1) and go through it chapter by chapter. As an intro to physics student, you probably only covered 20-30 of the 45+ chapters that this book contains. Now that you're earning a physics degree, you should know everything in this book. Go through the whole thing now and learn anything you didn't already know. Write down any formulas or definitions that you didn't remember, and also write down any representative examples. As many as 2/3 of the test questions can be answered with the information contained in this one book, so take as much time as you can to study this one.

Third Step. Go through your more advanced undergraduate books. Broad strokes here are OK: go through your E&M, classical mechanics, and statistical mechanics books and write down anything you didn't remember – maybe one idea from each section. Also brush up on math, especially calc III/vector theory, and linear algebra. In quantum, look through just the first two or three chapters of your book.

Fourth Step. Go through the practice exams. ETS provides a practice exam and has released four real exams that you can find (with solutions) pretty easily on the internet. Go through these as thoroughly as you can. Use your notes.

Fifth Step. In the days before the exam, memorize your notes.

Let me also share some hints for *taking* this test:

- The guessing penalty is such that you won't lose or gain any points for guessing randomly (I leave it as an exercise to the reader to prove this). But, if you can eliminate one answer choice and guess randomly from the others, then guessing will have an overall positive impact on your score. If you can eliminate more than one answer, then so much the better.

- This test is rife with red herrings. If you've eliminated some answers and are going to guess among the remaining choices, you may wish to guess totally randomly in order to avoid red herrings.

- Pay attention to units. You can often eliminate several answer choices just by considering the units.

- You won't have a calculator. Before breaking out the long division, try doing an "order of magnitude calculation" – that's normally all that's needed.

- You will need to know constants, since many of the answers are numerical.

Now let me answer the next question: what if the exam is in a few days and you haven't even started studying yet? In this case, I refer you to section 7.1: I've outlined some of the fastest things you can learn/memorize to boost your score.

2.4 Research Experience

Research experience is generally the most important component of your application. I should stress from the beginning that research experience means *doing* research, not just being present when research is done. Jobs working in the storeroom, mixing chemicals, or working for safety committees are nice jobs in that they pay the bills, but they will not, in general, be considered research experience.

Similarly, research courses will in general not count. Most undergraduate research courses mean doing a series of controlled experiments resulting in everyone turning in the same lab report – that's not research. Very advanced, open-ended research courses will count a little bit, but they are no replacement for actually doing real, useful, publishable[6] research under the guidance of a faculty member.

Finding Research Experience

Since you're going to grad school as the first step in a career doing research, I shouldn't have to convince you that doing research is a

---

[6]But don't get too caught up on publishing. Your research should eventually lead to something being published; beyond that, it's not necessary to worry about how many publications you have. The essential thing is that you're acquiring research skills

good idea. In fact, you'll want to do as much research as possible. For most students, the trouble is getting started.

Some undergraduate programs do a wonderful job of getting you involved in research. Sometimes they have courses where professors come in, announce that they're hiring, and tell you about all the interesting research projects that they are working on. In that case, you'll just want to take advantage of these programs.

In most schools, it's not that easy. Research is going on throughout the department, but it's not obvious how to get involved with it. First, you'll need to carefully consider what type of physics interests you (this will be your *subfield* – see section 4.5 for an extensive discussion about this). Then, you can go to your department's web site and find out which professors in your department are working in that subfield. Read through their webpages, and, if their research sounds interesting, send them an e-mail. These don't have to be particularly long or formal; something like the following is fine:

Dear Dr. Jones,
My name is Vincent Klug; I'm an undergraduate seeking some research experience. I'm most interested in Astrophysics, and I was reading on your website about your very interesting work related to accretion disks. Are you currently hiring undergraduates? If so, could I come by to discuss your research? Thanks very much.
-Vincent Klug

Some professors will ignore your e-mail, but most will respond, either offering an interview or with advice about who is hiring.

You're not restricted to working at your undergraduate school. For example, if you're going home for the summer, you can e-mail professors at the local university and see if anyone there would hire you for summer research. This is particularly useful if you're at a small school where there isn't much research going on: you can ask professors at another school to let you work with them.

If you're not too concerned about subfields, it's also OK to ask professors that you'd like to work for. Professors that you had for classes are great ones to start with.

Yet another option is a summer research program. There are many different varieties of these, such as SUROP or UROP, but perhaps the most prestigious is the REU – Research Experience for Undergraduates.[7] You'll go to a university (usually not your home university) for 10 weeks over the summer to do research full time. In exchange, you'll receive housing, meals, and a stipend. These usually are more "programs" than jobs: they also include lectures, social activities, etc. This is really a great deal: it's paid summer employment where you essentially get to spend your summer being a grad student. Moreover, there are quite a few of these programs,

---

[7]Though the expectations are much lower, applications for REU programs are very similar to applications for graduate school. As such, the techniques in chapter 4 will be relevant.

For REU applications, you apply to each program separately. An internet search for "NSF REU Physics" will lead you to a list of all schools that have received funding to host an REU program. You can then go to each program's website to apply.

and applications are free. If you submit enough applications, odds are that you'll be accepted somewhere even if your grades are not so good. Even the less competitive REU programs are still excellent research experience, and will really benefit your application.

Optimizing your research experience

So that's how you get research experience – now how do you get *the best* research experience? For one thing, you'll want to stick with the same subfield. It may seem like a good idea to try a bunch of different subfields so that you can choose the one you like best[8], but grad schools (unintentionally) penalize those who do so. Most applicants will be admitted based on the recommendation of a professor who was excited by your application: professors are more excited by applicants who have two years of work in the professor's subfield, and less so by applicants who worked in a dozen different subfields for two months each. So the first hint I can gave about optimizing your research experience is to get as much research experience as possible in a given subfield.

The second hint is to get interesting results. If two applicants both work equally hard in equally good labs but one has an interesting result to publish and talk about, that's the one whose career will go further. As a result, you should try to get a specific project that you can work on semi-independently. That way, even if you don't have enough to publish, you and your advisor will have something very specific you can talk about when you write your essays and your professor writes his/her letter of recommendation.

---

[8]This is actually a pretty unscientific paradigm, since no group is really representative of what the subfield is like.

Third, it is always interesting to have more than one research experience (within the same subfield). For example, working for two professors at two different schools within the same subfield is a great idea – it'll give you more experiences to chart on your CV and a better understanding of the subfield as a whole.

My fourth hint is to work for the right person. Working for a world-famous physicist is great if you can get it, but it is not necessary, nor should it take priority over finding someone with whom you're compatible. For example, a professor who micromanages can be either a blessing or a curse depending on your personality. You might not know your preferences yet, but you'll have a better idea after doing some research. This will be helpful when choosing your advisor in grad school!

Chapter 3

Where to Apply?

3.1 Factors to consider

The first question is always "does it matter where you go?" If you're applying to grad school straight out of college, the answer is a resounding yes. If you're hoping for a professorship or a position in a government lab, then my "yes" is even more emphatic.

Really, the only scenario in which it doesn't matter is if you're already employed and going back to earn a degree. In that case, you'll probably be so constrained by location that you'll only have a few options.

What factors should you consider when deciding where to apply?

- Quality and Reputation

- Presence of the subfield[1] you desire to study or might desire to study in the future

---

[1]See section 4.5 for more details about choosing a subfield

- Your compatibility with the program's environment

Notice what's *not* on this list. Location doesn't matter, or at least it shouldn't. Far too many short-sighted applicants refuse to apply to perfectly good schools in the Midwest and South. Money is also not on the list. All graduate programs pay terribly; deal with it.

Let me comment on why compatibility and reputation are so important. When applying for jobs after the PhD, you will be judged by the perceived quality of the research you've done. More reputable programs will give you more opportunity to do quality research; furthermore, your research will be taken much more seriously at a reputable program. Look at the faculty list at any school with a reputable physics department: about two-thirds of the professors will have attended a top-10 graduate school. On the other hand, if you're miserable, your research will suffer no matter where you are. It's important to get the best possible combination of reputation and happiness!

We keep using the word "reputation" – how exactly is that defined? There are approximately 170 physics graduate programs in the country. Their quality is ranked by two different agencies:

- *US News and World Report.* Every 2-4 years, *US News and World Report* sends out questionnaires to professors, industry leaders, and government lab leaders, asking them to give all programs a quality score between 1 and 5. Averaging these scores leads to a program ranking. This methodology is commonly criticized, but it's highly useful: it shows how your degree will be perceived by employers.

- *National Research Council.* This one is more scientific – it takes into account many variables including grants, publications, time to degree, student outcomes, student demographics, and many more factors, weighted appropriately. The result is an "range of probable ranks" which can be a little difficult to read.

Most applicants take these rankings far too seriously. For one thing, remember that I listed three factors to consider before: the rankings are only one. Second, you're going to working in a specific subfield, for which detailed rankings are not available (but would probably be quite different if they were). Third, a small difference in ranking doesn't mean much. Fourth, there is no "ideal" way to rank graduate schools, and you will find alarming variations from study to study.

What the rankings *are* good for is dividing the schools into tiers: the schools on each tier should be considered *equal*. Obviously the lines between each tier are very blurry, but as general guide, I will suggest dividing the schools into tiers like these:

- **1st Tier**: *Top-10 Programs.* These vary a little bit from year to year and ranking to ranking, but they are in general exactly who you'd expect: Harvard, MIT, Cal Tech, and Stanford, among others. The competition for these spots is ridiculous (admissions rates lower than 10%).

- **2nd Tier**: *Programs ranked 11-30.* These are in general large public universities, and the criteria for admission are just as high as the top-10 schools, though the competition is a little more reasonable (typically 20% or so). These programs should all be considered "excellent."

- **3rd Tier**: *Programs ranked 31-50.* These are in general mid-sized to large universities. The criteria for admission is a bit lower than in the higher tiers. These programs should all be considered "good."

- **4th Tier**: *Programs ranked 51-100.* Often, these departments are just as good as higher-ranked programs, but are just much smaller; others will have significantly fewer opportunities and resources. Admissions criteria for this tier are considerably lower.

- **5th Tier**. Unranked programs (those ranked below 100). The biggest problem with schools at this level is reputation: it can be very difficult to convince employers to take your qualifications seriously. The programs themselves are hit-or-miss – most are small departments with very limited research opportunities, but even this is fine if the opportunities available correspond to your interests. Others are growing programs, and a few are diploma mills. Proceed with caution!

Let me reiterate that all schools in a given tier are roughly equal – don't choose one school over another simply because the ranking is slightly higher!

One place you will consider is your undergraduate school. If your undergraduate school has a reasonable graduate program, it's probably worth an application since you have an excellent chance of being admitted there. However, you'll get a much more well-rounded

CV, better networking opportunities, and more research opportunities if you go somewhere different for your grad school. My advice is to apply to your undergraduate program, but not to accept that offer unless it's far and away the best offer you receive.

3.2   Where can I get in?

This is the hardest part. Remember that students are admitted at the convenience *of the department*. The problem is that different departments have different needs from year to year! As a result, there is no systematic way to approach this.

When answering the question "can I get into this school" the honest answer is usually "it depends." There are so many exceptions and special circumstances – both from the applicants and from the graduate schools – that it's really difficult to give firm guidelines. Unfortunately, "it depends" is a really useless answer, so I will reluctantly give some general guidelines for applications that will be competitive. Please don't take these guidelines as anything more than very, very very, very rough estimates.

Second Tier

Let's start with second tier schools. Your application is likely to be competitive if you have:

- a 3.75 QPA, especially in upper-division physics courses

- a PGRE score greater than 750 or so

- two years of interesting research experience, with a letter of recommendation from the advisor

These are very high standards, and second tier schools are pretty unforgiving in terms of mistakes. But even though the schools' *quality* should all be considered equal within this tier, the *competitiveness* varies wildly – often because uninformed applicants make bad decisions. Schools in the South and Midwest have fewer applicants; Ivy League schools have more (presumably because of name recognition). Larger programs accept more students, but usually do not have correspondingly more applicants. Even so, statistics, such as your grades, test scores, and number of years of research experience, matter the most at this tier.

First Tier

You might expect first tier schools to have even higher criteria, but this is in general not true. First tier schools have just about the same criteria, just lower acceptance rates. Since first tier schools are well-established as leading programs, they are less concerned about "statistics" like grades and research experience (these will still need to be excellent, in general, but they'll be less concerned about slight imperfections). Instead, they will choose those applicants that are the most interesting or seem subjectively like the "best fit." Many students are admitted at a professor's request. All of these schools have similar numbers of applicants (300-700), but some accept more students than others due to program size.

Third Tier

For third tier schools, competitive applications often have:

- a 3.50 QPA, especially in upper-division physics courses

- a PGRE score of around 700

- one year of interesting research experience, with good letters of recommendation

But these numbers are highly variable. If you have an "uneven" application, or statistics slightly lower than these, it's still well worth applying to a few of these programs; they can overlook quite a lot if you have something going for you. As in the second tier, competitiveness varies a lot here. Most students are doing the same analysis you are and coming to the same conclusions. You'll have better luck at the less obvious schools in this tier – those in less desirable locations or with less familiar names.

Fourth Tier

For fourth tier schools, competitive applications often have:

- a 3.0 QPA, but better if 3.25

- a PGRE score in low 600s, but better if 650+

- some interesting research experience beyond coursework *or* a very interesting research experience in elective coursework

Again, everyone is doing the same thing you're doing, and coming to the same conclusions. Many students think, "Well, if I have to go to a school in this tier, I'll at least go to one in this tier, I'll at least go to one in *this* particular location or with *this* particular name" and so these schools are unusually competitive.

Fifth Tier

For fifth tier schools, the criteria range wildly. Here are some rough guidelines:

- a 2.5 QPA, but much better if 3.0; hopefully physics grades are better than other grades

- PGRE often not required, high 500s is usually good enough if it is required

- any research experience is a bonus

- general GRE scores matter more here: scores of $165/150/4.0$ will be a help (but lower may be fine too)

3.3　Making your list

How many applications?

The first question is this: how many schools should you apply to? Applying to less than five is a terrible decision: random fluctuations might leave you shut out. Further, it's very unlikely that you'll get into one of your reach schools if you only apply to one reach school! So five is a good lower bound; I would suggest fifteen for an upper bound. Ten is pretty typical; twelve is a lot; by fifteen, the paperwork, fees, and letters of recommendation will be so voluminous that you will either forget something, run out of money, or estrange those who are writing your letters.

When you read the previous section, was it obvious which tier your statistics correspond to? If so, then you are unlikely to be surprised by any decisions: choose two reach schools, two reasonable schools, two safety schools and be done. If your statistics are mismatched (lots of research with bad grades, for example[2]) then each school will react a little differently – and you might want to apply to more schools. If there's something extremely unusual about your application, then each program can react even more differently, and I recommend applying to even more programs.

In addition to choosing a number of programs to apply to, you also want to think about how to distribute those applications.

- Reach schools: 1-4 schools that you think you have almost no chance of being admitted to. Don't do ones that are completely impossible, but choose ones that would be very surprising if you were to get in.

- "Maybe" schools: 1-8 schools that you think probably won't admit you. If you apply to many programs, this is where you want to add schools: most of them will be rejections, but hopefully you'll get lucky and one will admit you.

- "Probably" schools: 1-5 schools that you think probably will admit you.

- Safety schools: 2 schools that you think will definitely admit you. These should be ranked *well* below your other programs – if you miscalculate, you don't want to be shut out of grad school altogether.

---

[2]It's worth mentioning that the reverse is somewhat less endearing. Excellent coursework suggests that you'll get through the graduate coursework OK (which is true of most applicants); excellent research suggests that you'll have a very interesting dissertation, which is much more unusual.

A good rule of thumb is that people who do a good job making their lists get about 50% acceptances. If your list is very long, it might be closer to 30% or 40% (since you'll be adding "maybe schools" and reach schools, not safeties).

Making a "long list" and narrowing it down

After choosing a number, you'll want to take a ranked list of graduate programs. You can immediately cross off those programs that are ranked too high or too low, leaving yourself with 30-100 schools for 5-15 applications. This is your "long list" of potential places to apply. Now you'll want to gather information about each and every remaining program. Go to every single website and write down statistics. How many professors do they have that you'd be interested in working with? Are any admissions statistics available (some post recommended values for test scores, etc.)? What kind of topics are being studied that you find interesting? Is the program's size and location acceptable to you? Keep in mind that everyone is going through the same process as you and coming to much the same conclusions – so schools that appeal to you but seem less obvious might be better choices.

Making a "short list"

Proceed in this manner until you've narrowed it down to about twice the number you want. At this point, you'll want to start asking around: ask professors at your school, talk to current grad students at your school, and go to online forums and get information. Many schools list their graduate students on their website with their e-mail addresses: you can e-mail students in the prospective program with specific questions (if the e-mail addresses are not listed online, you can e-mail the graduate secretary and ask for the contact information of a current graduate student). If you're not sure about getting in, you can write a *brief* "will my application be competitive" e-mail to a member of the admissions committee (professors are often more helpful than the graduate secretary on this topic).

Chapter 4

Writing your Application

Now that you're under the gun, it's too late to become a better candidate: it's time now to *seem* like a better candidate. This chapter will take you through the actual application process. You can start using this chapter as early as the summer before your senior year.

When you're ready to start the application process, you will go to the website of your prospective school's physics department and find their application. About 10% of schools still have paper applications which you will print out, fill out, and mail in. The rest have moved to an online application system – these are nice because you will be able to verify whether your application is complete. A complete application is normally a few forms, three letters of recommendation[1], an essay or two, a CV, and a transcript.

---

[1]On an online application, you'll type in the name of your recommenders and the program will automatically e-mail those recommenders on your behalf. Therefore, don't type in your recommenders names until they have agreed to write for you! See section 4.2 for more details about letters of recommendation.

As you're filling out the application, it's important to realize that, at most schools, your application will actually be reviewed by two different bodies: the physics department, and the graduate school.[2] What normally happens is that the graduate secretary in the physics department compiles all your application materials. In January, the admissions committee (which consists entirely or mostly of physics professors) will come together and look over all the applications. They will then choose who to accept and who to decline. If you're accepted, you'll receive an e-mail[3] telling you that you have been tentatively accepted. As a result, you'll want to orient your application with respect to a highly qualified physics professor, not some clown in the graduate school.

The clowns in the graduate school get your application next. If you're rejected, you'll probably get the letter from the graduate school rather than the physics department. If you're tentatively accepted by the physics department, you still have to be confirmed by the graduate school. This is normally a red stamp, but it can be a real problem if you have immigration problems, a record of academic misconduct, poor English skills, unusually low grades, or a criminal record. The physics department's standards are almost always higher than those of the graduate school, but there are occasionally things that the physics professors won't care about, but the graduate school will. To that end, you should be sure to address any such problems in your application.

[2]A particular university's "graduate school" is responsible for graduate students in all the departments at that university. The physics department generally has a separate, parallel admissions process; you'll have to be admitted into both the graduate school and the physics department.

[3]usually – some schools still use US mail; others make phone calls

4.1 Timeline

Here's an ideal timeline for the entire application process.

Summer before senior year

- Sign up for the general GRE and the Physics GRE.

- Choose a list of schools to apply to.

- Choose three (or four!) professors to write a letter of recommendation for you.

- Write a Curriculum Vitae and a Statement of Purpose.

September & October

- Take the general GRE.

- Take the Physics GRE at the end of October.

- Ask your professors to write you letters of recommendation.

- Work on your applications for the schools that have the earliest deadlines, and those in the middle of your list.

November

- Once your Physics GRE scores come in, finalize your list of schools to apply to.

- Request transcripts be sent to all your schools.

- Request additional score reports for the GRE as needed.

- Remind your professors that letters of recommendation are needed.

- Continue working on your applications

December and January

- Finish the rest of the applications, and pay the application fees

- In the days before the deadlines pass, make sure your professors have provided letters of recommendation. Pester them as much as necessary.

February and March

- As application results come in, you'll be invited to visit some programs. If you are seriously considering accepting an offer of admission, you should definitely accept their offer to visit the campus.

- Decline all offers as soon as you know that you will not be attending.

April

- If you have not already accepted an offer, make sure to accept before the April 15 deadline. Decline all other offers.

- If you want to start research over the summer, talk to professors to see if anyone is hiring.

- After your degree is conferred, send your final transcript to the graduate program.

- If possible, it's always nice to tell your recommenders about your decision. A small gift is also appropriate at this time, especially if you asked for many letters of recommendation.

4.2   Letters of Recommendation

You will almost always need three letters of recommendation. The worst-case scenario for these letters is that you get three professors who all say very vague things and give you a "non-committal" letter of recommendation.[4] That's actually a significant achievement – finding three professors who know you well enough to write you a letter and give you a positive recommendation is not an easy task, and you will get some credit for having done so. Nonetheless, this puts you at a huge disadvantage since most other applicants will have positive, detailed recommendations.

The best-case scenario involves three letters distributed as such:

1. Your first letter comes from your research advisor. He or she describes many specific contributions you've made to the group and skills you've picked up along the way.

2. Your second letter comes from either another research advisor or a professor who taught you in a few classes. He or she can describe how you stand out from the other students and confirm the first recommender's appraisal of your abilities.

---

[4]Technically, the worst case scenario is that they use their letters to torch you, but most professors will simply refuse to write rather than torch you. If in doubt, it's entirely appropriate to ask them whether they could write a positive letter of recommendation

3. Your third letter comes from an out-of-department professor, maybe someone in math or chemistry – or maybe even a humanities professor. This person will lament the fact that you're not studying their field and point out your obvious brilliance.

4. Fourth letters are only occasionally accepted – if they are accepted, it would be nice to provide it. This letter could be from a professor who has a high regard for you personally, and can give the committee a touching statement about what a unique and talented individual you are.

Regardless of how your letters are distributed, it's important to give your professors lots of notice – ask them to write in late September, for example. For the most part, asking them is not something you want to rush through. You'll want to send them an e-mail along the lines of the following:

Dear Professor,

I very much enjoyed taking particle physics with you last semester, and hope very much to learn more about the subject. As a senior, I am thinking a great deal about my future in physics, and would like to request a brief meeting with you on this topic. If you have time for a meeting, please do let me know, I am free any day after 2:00. Thanks very much,

Vincent Klug

During the meeting, you should be direct – don't keep them guessing. Something like this is appropriate:

Thanks for meeting with me today. I asked for this meeting because I'm applying to graduate school to study particle physics. Since you taught the undergraduate particle physics class, and observed my work first hand, I was hoping that you'd be able to write a letter of recommendation for me. Obviously you would just be talking about the things you already know about me, but I've brought a CV and a transcript for background information. Do you think you'd be able to give me a good recommendation?

Your professor probably saw this coming the moment he/she read your e-mail, so don't be too nervous, and don't dilly-dally. Just explain that you're going to grad school and would like a letter.

Asking the professor can work differently if it's someone you know well – if you're asking your research advisor, for instance, it's OK to wait for an appropriate time, and then ask "Can I ask you about grad school?" Your research advisor should definitely be unsurprised by your request for a letter.

Conversely, if it's someone you don't know well at all, or if you know them well but aren't sure of their feelings for you, you might want to ask them about a letter via e-mail. Here's a sample:

Dear Professor,

I am writing to ask if you would be willing to recommend me for graduate school in theoretical physics. I've taken two classes with you and learned quite a lot, and I think that a letter from you would be very helpful to the admissions committee. I know that I didn't do very well in PHYS 303, and I understand if you are therefore unwilling to recommend me. However, I nonetheless learned quite a lot in that class, and I did much better in PHYS 401, which you also taught.

Normally I would ask you for a letter of recommendation in person, but I wanted to give you a chance to consider whether you can give me a positive recommendation. I'd be happy to come by your office to discuss this further: I will also give you a CV and a transcript for background information.

Thanks very much for considering this,

Vincent Klug

Some professors might be upset if you ask for a letter by e-mail, but most will get over it if you explain why you did so. But let me underline again to keep this e-mail brief; longer discussions with lots of detail are best done in person, or at least delayed until after the professor has had a chance to respond to your initial request.

Regardless of what you say to get them to agree, you should follow up with them immediately by e-mail. You can use this section to drop hints as well as more practical information. For example:

Dear Professor,

Thank you for agreeing to write a letter of recommendation for me. Others professors will be able to talk about my research, but I feel that you're the one who can best discuss my interest in graphene layers, and my aptitude for computer programming.

All the schools I'm applying to have online applications, and I've given all of them your name. You should soon be receiving requests for letters for six schools: MIT, Harvard, Texas-Austin, UCSD, Florida, and Iowa State. I gave you a CV and transcript this morning as background materials; I've also attached those, along with a statement of purpose, to this e-mail. Thanks again for writing for me; I'll let you know of any good news.
Vincent Klug.

Now professors usually put off writing these letters until the last possible moment, so it's a good idea to send them follow up reminders as the deadline approaches. I suggest sending one a week from the deadline, another 2-3 days from the deadline, and a last one on the morning of the deadline. This last one, if necessary, should use capital letters and the word "urgent" several times. Needless to say, you should be checking your application websites to see if the letters have been submitted – don't send them reminder e-mails if they've already written for you.

Let me end this section with a list of DONT's:

- Don't be afraid of getting rejected. Professors are used to telling people that they can't write a positive letter – such conversations can be awkward, but it's not a big deal. It's much better to ask and be told no than to not ask.

- Don't expect them to say yes. Professors spend their entire lives building reputations for themselves, and won't put them on the line for just any student who asks. In particular, the professor is under no obligation at all to write a letter.

- Don't assume that professors have good things to say. This isn't necessarily malicious – they might think they're doing you a favor by writing a bad or mediocre recommendation, as your application will be incomplete unless you have three recommenders. You can specifically ask, "Are you able to write a positive recommendation for me, or would it be better if I asked someone else?"

- Do not ask to read the letter. This is inappropriate. Professors are expected to write their letters candidly, without having to explain themselves to you. To that end, you will be asked on your application whether you wish to waive your legal right to read the letter after you matriculate. You should waive this right.[5]

- Do not ask them to write a letter on two days notice. You should give at least 2-3 weeks notice. If you do have to give less notice, you should be very apologetic.

- Do not be afraid to pull the plug on an unpromising letter. If a professor agrees to write, but then avoids your follow-ups or hints that he/she is having trouble thinking of good things to say, you should send a quick e-mail thanking him/her for considering you, and telling him/her that you've found another recommender.

---

[5]Though intended to increase transparency in the admission process, the "Family Educational Rights and Privacy Act" (FERPA) only allows you to see your application (including your letters of recommendation) at the school to which you matriculated. Since most students are only interested in reading the letters if they were not admitted, there's really no reason you shouldn't waive your right to view these letters.

- Do not list people without first contacting them, even if you're sure that they would be willing to recommend you.

- Don't be alarmed if the professor asks you to read the letter before it is submitted (even if you waived your rights to read it) or even if he/she asks you to write a first draft of your own letter. Professors are busy, and there's nothing unethical about giving him/her detailed notes (in draft form) or help proofreading. On the other hand, I would argue that it is unadvisible to forge your recommender's signature or to file a letter that your recommender has not read, even if you have his/her permission to do so. Obviously, submitting a letter on your professor's behalf without permission could lead to expulsion and legal action, both from the graduate school and from the professor.

4.3　Statement of Purpose

If you ask a member of the admissions committee about the statement of purpose, they'll say something like the following:

Naïve statement: Well, most of them are only glanced at, since most are absolutely terrible. Well-written ones can be read carefully, but ultimately they don't factor that much into the decision unless they give us new information.

Physics department faculty pride themselves on being objective, so they will be reluctant to realize that a well-written statement of purpose can really make a big difference. As a result, this statement is not all that accurate – your statement of purpose can really have an impact. Why?

- There are already many applicants and few spots. If your statement of purpose is horrible, they will consider only your statistics – which might not be enough. But if you statement of purpose is compelling, they will often try to find a spot for you even if you don't have the best statistics in the pool.

- Most statements of purpose are absolutely horrible (probably because lazy applicants start writing them the night before the deadline). If yours is even halfway decent, it will stand out from the pack.

- Your statement of purpose is the one part of your application over which you have complete control. It's your chance to frame your application the way you want it framed: emphasizing the good and minimizing the bad.

On that note, let me define exactly what a statement of purpose is:

Definition. A *statement of purpose* is an essay, usually two single-spaced pages or less, which outlines why you are applying to grad school by way of discussing your interests and experiences.

A typical statement of purpose will start by explaining your love of physics and/or your interest in a particular type of physics, proceed to discussing your research experience, coursework, and/or other relevant details, and conclude that attending grad school is a reasonable decision.

Now you're probably thinking that the statement of purpose is just one more annoying thing in a long list of annoying things you to have do in order to complete your application. I disagree: you're going to need to write short, clear, well-written papers like this over and over again during your career. If you have the time,[6] you should take a week or two to really learn how to do this type of writing – you'll acquire a useful skill and you'll end up with an excellent statement of purpose.

I strongly suggest that you write your statement of purpose during the summer before your senior year; that way you'll have enough time to really write this properly. Let me outline your ideal writing process:

1. Look over sample admissions essays with commentary. This will give you an idea of what you're aiming for.

2. Write down your goals for the statement of purpose. What specific information do you want to give? What weaknesses in your application do you want to strengthen?

3. Form your goals into an outline.

4. Write a first draft – this may require many incomplete first drafts before you finally have a complete essay.

5. Revise. This is the part that should take the longest. It's not unusual (in fact, it's highly recommended) to spend a few hours revising, then throw away your entire essay and write a new first draft.

6. Proofread carefully.

---

[6]If you *don't* have the time, you should still read this section, but you might have to skip a few of the steps. I also direct you to chapter 7: I put in a sample outline and some sample essays that may speed things up.

7. Format your final text.

Following this algorithm, you will begin by looking at sample admissions essays and reading through the editor's commentary. This is *really* worth the effort: you can't write a good essay until you know how it will be evaluated (think about your physics coursework – examples are always more helpful than theorems). I include two sample essays (with commentary) in section 7.4, but in order to really get the hang of writing these, you will probably find it most helpful to get a book with dozens and dozens of examples with commentary.

The problem will be finding such a book: I am not aware of any designed for science grad students. There are a few designed for graduate school in general, but these can be very misleading: their tricks might succeed in dazzling the clowns in the admissions office, but they will not impress the physics professors that will be evaluating your application.

As a result, I recommend getting one of the books that helps you write an *undergraduate* admission essay (see sec. 7.1 for a recommendation). While the specific prompts and goals for such essays are different than those for your graduate statement of purpose, the techniques are transferable. Further, such books generally have helpful, specific advice for brainstorming and tweaking your essay, which will be helpful later on.

The second step is to write a list of goals for these essays. For example, you may want your statement to convince the committee that you're hard-working, that getting that C in mechanics was a fluke, that your research experience is more significant than it looks, etc. In addition to your goals, you're obliged to comment on your research experience, your coursework, and the reason you want to do physics – so think of any related stories or philosophies that you want to share with the committee. Don't worry about length or cohesiveness yet, just write down as many things as you can.

The third step is to combine everything you have into a workable outline. Remember that you should start with something interesting: it's most common to start with an anecdote, but anything to capture your reader's interest is fine. You won't end with a "conclusion" per se, but you will need to tie your essay together somehow. The two most common tactics for concluding are to organize your essay chronologically, ending with your desire to go to this particular graduate school, or to come full circle, returning to an idea brought up in your first sentence.

Now it's time for a first draft. Unless you have a brilliant idea for an opening, start with the second sentence of the first paragraph. Then follow your outline as you fill out the essay. This is the "do or die" time for your essay – if you still haven't gotten anywhere after an hour, throw everything away and start over again with a new outline.

After you get a first draft, it's just a matter of revising and formatting your essay until it's something you're happy with. This should take a significant amount of time – compare your essays to those in the "writing an admissions essay" book from step one.

The last step is to format your final document. *Unless otherwise instructed*, you should have a single-spaced document with one inch margins and full alignment. Use a blank line to separate your paragraphs. You should also have a header that indicates your name, application number (if you're given one), current department, and prospective department.

Let me end this section with some specific advice and common traps.

What you don't want

Consider the following statement of purpose:

Ever since I was 11, I have experienced a fascination with the tactile world. Sometimes I lay awake at night thinking, where did everything come from? I am constantly struck by the wonder of creation. In middle school, I won first place for my science fair entry about "what makes plants grow quickly?" Since then, my tradition of excellence has continued, leading to my decision to devote my entire life to science, a subject about which I am passionate. I hope to do this at your amazing school.....

What do you think? Sounds pretty good, right? The author is passionate about science, curious, and apparently has a tradition of excellence.

Wrong! First, the author has spent about eighty words – 15% of the entire essay! – and I've learned almost nothing. I am indeed convinced that the author is passionate about science, but I had surmised as much in view of his/her completion of an undergraduate science degree and application to a PhD program. In fact, the only real fact I didn't already know is that this student did a successful middle school project about botany – an accomplishment in which I am entirely uninterested.

In addition, I don't buy it. I have known many scientists, and none of them lay awake at night thinking "where did everything come from?" Curiosity is a very good thing, but at this level, I would hope to see a bit more sophistication.

Third, this author uses a lot of puffery with no facts. I am convinced that the author is passionate about science, so the "about which I am passionate" line is unnecessary. However, I am not sure why the applicant is convinced that my school is "amazing", why his/her "tradition" is so "excellent", or what exactly he/she finds so "fascinating."

If I were on the committee, I would stop reading at this point. I had (implicitly) asked the applicant a perfectly simple, reasonable question: "what is your purpose in applying to this program?" Such a reasonable question deserves a reasonable answer, not an crazy monologue, complete with a discussion about childhood idiosyncrasies and "fascination with the tactile world."

Getting Started

- Do not begin with a boring story about your childhood, the upshot of which is that you were really interested in physics. This is done very often, and it's just as yawn-inducing every time.

- Do not give a boring story about how you witnessed an everyday event, and got thinking about why it happened, and thus decided to study physics. Again, this is extremely common and rather unconvincing.

- Do not give vague generalities about when you "fell in love with physics." This does not make you sound passionate, just unoriginal.

Rather than resorting to one of these lame openings, you should really ask yourself why you think a career as a research physicist is a good idea. There might not be a good story – perhaps you just love solving problems, or love using math all the time, or you like the lifestyle of a physicist. Perhaps there's something you learned that you found very interesting, or a particular research project was so enjoyable that you want to do more. These are perfectly good reasons; moreover, the professors reading your application are in the field for similar reasons, and will relate to you. Also bear in mind:

- Don't start with a dictionary definition, song lyrics, a quote, or onomatopoeia. This is overdone (*unless* you confound expectations, such as by starting with a quote that doesn't make any sense).

- Don't start with something boring, like "This is my statement of purpose" or "My name is ..." While these are not laughable, they are also not much of a "hook."

Beginning the statement of purpose is the most difficult part! As a result, most begin with as above, with some unconvincing and clichéd opening. Here's a few things you can try instead:

- Try telling a real, recent, brief, interesting story.

- Try describing something you feel strongly about, or something you do regularly out of principle.

- Try stating something obvious in a new or provocative way.

- Try stating something non-obvious in a casual way.

- Try to incorporate humor (but don't overdo it. Colleges love the idea of admitting a clown, but grad schools are more cautious.)

Writing the Body

After you've gotten started, you'll want to address your goals, research experiences, and coursework experiences, and your reasons for applying to the program itself. But:

- Don't repeat the CV. You should use this to expand on the CV, such as by giving examples of research projects you've done with positive results, situations that have challenged your or that demonstrate your philosophy, or so forth.

- Don't comment on the school's location or compensation. By applying, you have indicated that those characteristics are acceptable to you.

- It's okay to be honest. For example, if you're applying to Harvard, the reason you're applying is because it has an excellent reputation. Don't pretend like you're unaware of this. Similarly, if you're overqualified for a program, it's okay to admit that (if it comes up – don't go out of your way to mention this!)

One reason most applications are so "horrible" is that they all tell the same boring, clichéd stories described above. The other reason is that they are poorly edited. To this end:

Editing Techniques

- Go through each paragraph and write down (actually write it down) the central idea of the paragraph. Then compile this into an outline. Does the outline make sense? Did you cover everything you wanted to cover? Compare it to this original outline you wrote in step 2.

- Go through each paragraph sentence by sentence, and ask yourself "What does this sentence contribute to the paragraph?" If it doesn't contribute anything, kill it.

- Make sure you have transitions between paragraphs. These can be "Also," or "Secondly, " like you learned in elementary school, but they can also be more detailed, such as "My initial impressions of astrophysics were backed up by the astrophysics classes I took, in particular observational astrophysics during my junior year."

- Use a variety of sentence lengths. You don't want every sentence to be long and complicated.

- Be concise. Long sentences have to "pull their weight" by contributing a lot to your essay. If your long sentences don't contribute much, shorten them.

- Read the essay through several times, slowly and out loud. Let it "cool" for a couple hours, then read it slowly again. Any awkward or unclear constructions should be fixed. Get someone else to read over it too.

- Make absolutely certain there are no spelling or grammar errors. Everyone thinks this is obvious and is certain they have not made any mistakes; yet, most essays do contain simple mistakes with spelling and grammar.

- Do not punch up the language with a thesaurus. Thesauri are useful if you don't want to keep using the same word over and over again. They should not be used just because you're pretending to have a broad vocabulary.

- Do not use clichés.

- Count how many important things you've told the reader that they did not already know and could have not guessed. This should be a pretty high number!

- Don't worry about word counts until the end. Your first draft (depending on your writing style) will probably naturally come out to 2-3 pages. After editing described above (and more aggressive editing for length, if needed), it will be around two full pages: that's the desired length. Some schools will request a shorter statement of purpose; you can cut down the full-length one as needed. But notice that you start with a long essay and then cut it down; don't try to write something that's the right length the first time (it'll get shorter during editing, then you'll be trying to think of things to add).

- Aggressive editing for length is often a good thing, as it makes your essay much cleaner. You'll probably get the length you need just by eliminating unnecessary words, or replacing complicated sentences with shorter, simpler ones.

4.4   Curriculum Vitae

Your curriculum vitae is typically a 1-3 page document,[7] on which you will list all of your qualifications to be a grad student. Writing this is quick and easy, so I'll just take you through the various parts of the CV. I also include a sample CV in the appendices.

Heading

You should put your name, address, and e-mail address at the top of the CV. Your name should be centered; feel free to use bold, capital letters, and/or a distinctive font. This is the one time in your life as a physicist that you can go nuts with fonts and margins, so have fun with it. Your address and e-mail address should be placed above or below your name in an attractive way.

Objective

You should clearly label this section (and all subsequent sections) – put the word "Objective" (or alternatively "Career Objective," "Profile," or "Personal Statement") in bold or underline right below

---

[7]At this stage. Your professors' CVs are probably much longer.

your heading. This should be just 1-3 sentences describing your objectives. You should mention your desire to get into a graduate school, do research (in a particular subfield, if applicable), and further your coursework. If you have a particular career in mind, you can mention that here as well.

Education

List your undergraduate institution(s), major(s) and minor(s), and any elective upper-division or honors program courses. If you graduated with honors (*cum laude*) you can mention that here; you should also list your QPA and test scores if they are high enough.

Research Experience

This section list all research positions you've held, with a brief description of each. Your description can be a short paragraph or 3-4 bullet points. You should include your supervisor, the location, the subfield, the skills you used, and any interesting results.

Teaching Experience

If you have any teaching experience, you should list it here. Include your title, the courses taught, and the number of students taught. If you have no teaching experience, omit this section.[8]

---

[8]By the by, don't expect teaching experience to be a huge help. Although you will spend your first year or two teaching classes, most programs could absolutely care less about any experience or interest you have in teaching (unless your subfield of interest is "physics education.")

Administrative Experience

If you have any administrative experience, such as being a secretary in a scientific setting, serving on committees, holding elected positions, or so forth, you should list them here. You can also call this "leadership experience" if appropriate. If you have no such experiences, omit this section.

Publications

If any of your work has been published, you should cite yourself here.

Extra-Curricular Activities

If you have any relevant extra-curricular activities, you can list them here. In general, you should only do so if you held an elected or founding position, if the extra-curricular is a sport (college sports generally involve a significant time commitment), or if the activity is related to science.

Awards

If you've won any awards in college, you should list them here. Include the name of each award and why you won it. If you haven't won any awards, omit this section.

Skills

If you have any particular skills, you should list them here. These might include languages you speak, computer software you know (advanced scientific software only), computer languages you know, and any scientific equipment that you're familiar with (lasers, electronics, telescopes, etc.), among others. If you have no such skills, you can omit this section.

References

If you have people who could recommend you that did not write a letter, you may wish to list their contact information on your CV.

Work Experience

If you've already had a career in science – or if you're returning to school after any sort of career – then you should list your work experience on your CV. If you're coming straight from college, though, I do *not* recommend adding a "work experience" section: working at McDonald's is not going to make you a better grad student. If you think this experience *is* relevant to your application, you can mention it in your statement of purpose or, if it exists, in your "diversity statement" – I'll discuss the diversity statement in section 4.6.

Other Sections

You can add other sections as needed.

4.5 Choosing a Subfield

There are different types of physicists: each physicist has a particular specialty, a *subfield* that he/she specializes in.

This may be a totally new concept to you, so let me give three definitions here.

Definition. *Paradigm* refers to how data is collected. The main paradigms are experimental, theoretical, and (according to some) computational.

Definition. *Subject* refers to what type of physics is studied. There are many different subjects, but perhaps the most common are astrophysics, biophysics, condensed matter physics, and particle physics.

Definition. *Subfield* refers to a combination of paradigm and subject (for example, theoretical condensed matter physics)

On your application, you will be asked to state the subfield that you desire to study. This is important for two reasons:

- Certain advisors are looking for graduate students; others are not. The program wants to make sure that the interests of the incoming graduate class loosely correspond to the interests of the professors who will take on graduate students.

- Your research experience will be evaluated based on your stated subfield of interest.

This last bullet point is particularly important. What often happens during graduate school admissions is this:

1. First, your application is looked over by holistically by the entire committee, and any obvious choices are made. Un-qualified students are rejected and very-qualified students are

given early offers and fellowships.

2. Everyone else (and this is at least 50% of the applicants) are considered qualified to attend, but there are not enough spots. These applications are then staffed out by subfields: professors in each subfield will look through those applications and determine who they want to fight for. Things like grades and test scores do still matter, but these professors will be most interested in your application if you have lots of relevant research experience.

As a result, you should continue with the same subfield that you studied as an undergraduate. If you have lots of research experience in biophysics, for example, but you list astrophysics as your area of interest, then you'll likely be admitted only at the request of an astrophysics professor. Astrophysics professors won't be very excited by your application if you don't have any relevant research experience!

That's not to say that you shouldn't change subfields if you want to. If you're pondering a switch, I suggest listing both areas as potential areas of interest. You should also use your statement of purpose to address the reason for your interest in both subfields.[9]

As I mentioned before, it can be difficult at this stage to proceed if your research experience is non-homogeneous. In this case, you

---

[9]By the way, don't worry too much about choosing the correct subfield; students often change subfields during grad school. You should know, though, that switching earlier is better. Switching during the first or second year will barely affect your progress; switching during the fourth year might delay your graduation by two or more years, since you'll have to restart your research.

should mention your variety of research experiences in your statement of purpose. For one thing, you can emphasize that you've already experienced many types of physics and so you're very committed to the area you chose. That can be a real selling point: every year, many students are admitted because their interests correspond to the program's needs, but then their interests shift to something less convenient.

Now you may not have done much research, in which case it can be difficult to choose a subfield. It doesn't really matter much in any case (your subfield preference won't count for much without any research) but this is a good opportunity to give some thought to your choice.

Choosing a Paradigm

Let's discuss each paradigm. Experimental physics means collecting data through experiment, then analyzing that data. For astrophysics, this paradigm is called "observational," for obvious reasons. In terms of day-to-day work, experimental physicists spend most of their research hours in the lab (individually or in small groups) building experiments to collect data. They typically use high-powered and expensive equipment (such as lasers or microscopes) and are required to publish so many papers per year. Things are a little different in astrophysics and particle physics. Observational astrophysicists spend their time building and looking through telescopes; experimental particle physicists work in very large international collaborations instead of small groups. Experimental physics has a few advantages: for one thing, you will almost certainly get some results (even if only negative results) and you'll therefore be able to publish something. For another thing, experimental physicists have many career opportunities: the majority of professorships, lab appointments, and industry positions are for experimental physicists.

Theoretical physics usually means making some assumption, then running simulations to explore the consequences of that assumption, eventually resulting in a prediction which can be compared to experimental results. Some of these assumptions (such as string theory) result in quite complicated models that are virtually impossible to test experimentally. In terms of day-to-day work, theoretical physicists spend most of their time on the computer, writing code to explore these possibilities. Theoretical physicists are generally very happy with their jobs, but you should be aware that job opportunities for theorists are rare. Even in graduate school, you'll probably have to teach most of the time in order to support yourself. An often-quoted statistic is that ten years after earning the PhD, only 10% of theorists are employed as theoretical research physicists.[10]

A third, emerging paradigm is computational physics – this involves reducing physics problems (very complicated ones, with thousand-

---

[10]I've never been able to run down a source for this fact, or the equivalent statistic for experimental physicists. Anecdotally, though, it seems about right: I can also anecdotally assure you that the number for experimentalists is much higher, though I won't hazard a guess at a number.

Don't be overly alarmed by this percentage: not all students who earn PhDs in theoretical physicists *want* to get a job as a theoretical research physicist! They also have excellent career opportunities working for industries outside of physics, such as in the financial or defense sectors.

term-Hamiltonians for example) to something that can be solved quickly by computers. This paradigm is still emerging: some consider it a subject rather than a paradigm; still others consider it a particular type of theoretical physics.

It is a very good idea to specify a paradigm, even if you haven't chosen a subject (conversely, you can specify a subject but not a paradigm – that's equally good). Many advise students "on the borderline" to go with experimental physics due to the higher job security and funding levels. However, both experimental and theoretical physics require specific interests and aptitudes, and you'll want to think candidly about whether or not they match up with your own.

Choosing a Subject

I've already mentioned the four most common subfields above: astrophysics, biophysics, condensed matter physics, and particle physics.[11] If you have no idea which subfield to go with, I suggest choosing one of these, since these areas of interest are available at most departments.

Astrophysics, as you've probably guessed, means studying space. It requires just as much math as any other branch of physics (that's a common misconception) and can require unusual work hours (observing at night is common). You'll also be using a lot of software specifically designed for astronomers.

---

[11]For a more complete list, see section 7.1

Biophysics, as you may have guessed, means applying the tools of physics (such as quantum and statistical mechanics) to biological systems. This subject has only recently become accepted as a mainstream branch of physics, and so there are lots of job openings in this field. Further, this is perhaps the only mainstream area of physics where all the "easy stuff" has not already been done. The techniques used in biophysics are very similar to condensed matter physics.

Condensed matter physics generally involves studying particle-particle interactions, such as those found in solids and liquids. It is closely related to chemistry, but physicists tend to look at these phenomena from the lens of quantum and statistical mechanics rather than considering the interactions of the particular chemical species involved.

Particle physics involves studying the particles that constitute all matter. Working at smaller and smaller distance scales requires higher and higher energy scales, so particle physics is generally done in teams ranging from several dozen to several thousand collaborators (this is something to consider when choosing your subject). Theoretical particle physics is less collaborative than experimental.

I mentioned earlier that experimental is easier than theoretical in terms of both admission to grad school and career prospects after graduation. Similarly, some subjects are more competitive than others. These very *a lot* by school – but on a national scale, the most competitive subfield is widely believed to be particle theory.

Many of the smaller subjects listed in section 7.2 (such as mathematical physics) are also quite competitive since there are so few job openings in those subjects.

I'll wrap up this section by answering the most common question: what do I do if I have no idea what I want to study? If you've done research in a particular area, claim that you will continue with that same area (this is probably true, and will help with admissions). If you have no research experience and no clear idea of what to study, don't just guess randomly. Committees can see through that (even if they don't see through it, it won't help your application and it may even hurt your application). Instead, state an undecided subfield, and discuss any preferences you do have in your statement of purpose.

4.6   Everything Else

Early Admissions

You should submit your application before the deadline. Some schools do not give a firm deadline but rather a "range of dates when applications will be accepted." In this case, you should treat the earliest such date as a deadline. Grad schools do not have "early decision" in the way that undergraduate programs do.

Late Admissions

Every year, students realize in April that they have not applied anywhere. There is no easy way to deal with this situation; you'll need to look for programs that accept late applications – of which there are few. It might be easiest to simply e-mail every single program on your long list (see section 3.3) and ask if they will accept an application. The odds are that you'll have to reapply during the next admissions cycle.

Diversity Statements

Many schools require an additional essay on the topic of diversity. In what ways will you contribute to the diversity of the program? What adversity have you overcome in your life? This essay is often optional.

This essay will be read by the physics admissions committee, but it really won't affect the decision unless there's new information here. Obviously you should comment on any obstacles you have overcome; if you happen to be a political prisoner refugee from West Africa, this would be a great time to mention it! But don't blow hot air – if you're a white middle-class male, it won't hurt your application too much if you neglect this optional essay.

If your background is a little less interesting, there are still some things you might be able to comment on (depending on how the prompt is phrased). What other interests do you have, outside of physics? Did you have any intellectual or developmental challenges? Maybe you went to a small school (for a good reason), and had extra challenges getting research experience? Did you have financial difficulties paying for college – maybe you paid your own way, or worked a job all the way through? Do you have an interesting background with respect to gender, ethnicity, race, religion or sexual orientation?

Other places you applied

Most applications ask you about where else you applied. This is generally optional; it is acceptable to leave this blank or to say "contact me to discuss." It's generally considered acceptable to give a few examples of schools you applied, rather than listing all of them.

This section is mostly for the program's research rather than the evaluation of your application, but it can still have an impact. If you admit that you're applying to 25 schools, then statistics suggest that you'll be going somewhere else, and so they might not even bother to waste an offer of admission on you. Also, if you're a mediocre applicant but you claim that you only applied to MIT and Harvard, then they might question your judgment.

Transcripts

Most graduate programs will require an official or unofficial transcript from you. You can get these from your school's registrar's office; there may be a fee. You'll want to send these out as early as possible; if you have an online application, you should be able to verify that they arrived. After your Fall term ends, you should send an updated transcript if your Fall coursework went well.

Online presence

Programs occasionally do a Google search for your name. It's therefore a good idea to modify your Facebook page and clean up your website. Also, beware of leaving identifying information on grad school forums – it's perhaps a little overcautious, but some professors have admitted that they check these forums regularly to get a candid idea of what their applicants are thinking. In this vein, you should also record a professional voice mail message in case they call to request an interview.

Interested in Unfunded?

You may be asked whether you are interested in being accepted if the program cannot offer funding. Most applicants in physics programs answer no, but there's no reason not to answer honestly.

Fee Waiver

You can apply for a fee reduction or fee waiver. There's absolutely no down side to requesting this if the application fee provides a hardship for you. There are also some programs that offer fee reductions to those who have particular qualifications; this can save you a few bucks if you qualify.

Chapter 5

Results & Decisions

5.1   Grad School Visits

If you are not rejected, you will usually be invited to visit the campus. This normally comes after admission, but may come before admission in the form of an interview. The good news is these visits are usually paid for by the program.

The only difference between an interview and a visit is what you wear. If you've already been admitted, then you can wear whatever you want – but it's still a good idea to look nice, as you might be under consideration for fellowships or other perks. If the word "interview" is used, then you'll want to dress formally unless your letter states otherwise.

These visits, interview or otherwise, are a lot of fun – they are free trips around the country to tour college campuses and talk about physics. You'll have sessions with grad students and with professors in your subfield of interest. There are also social interactions – dinners, bowling, bar trips, parties, etc. Don't be afraid to have fun at these mixers, even if it is an interview: it's definitely a good thing if you interact well with the other grad students. This is perhaps the only interview in your life where it's acceptable (perhaps even encouraged) to drink alcohol!

This part of the process is pretty simple: you go to the meetings, hang out with the grad students, and see if it seems like a good fit. In addition to the "goodness of fit" you also want to look for a prospective advisor. It's a good idea to prepare for your visit by finding a list of advisors in your subfield whose work seems interesting to you. You'll want to meet with as many of these as possible during the visit: how many do you think you could work with? For example, there might be three professors whose work seems good on paper, but if one is about to retire and the other two are abusive, then the school might not be the best fit after all.

You'll be asked many times during your visit whether you have any questions. Here are some good questions you may want to ask:

- What is the overall yield, in terms of number of students accepted vs. number of students graduating with PhD? The graduate director should know this number cold; be suspicious if he or she refuses to provide it. As a rule of thumb, 30% of students will drop out of their own accord, so a 70% overall yield is about the most that can be expected.

- Where do students go after graduation? To what extent does the program help with placement into post-docs or careers?

- If you're interested in working with someone, ask whether they'll be accepting students out of your year. If you can't meet with someone that you're interested in working for, you can ask the other professors in the same subfield about that person's research.

- What are the qualifying exams like? What sort of material is tested? How many students fail the exam ever year? When are they taken? If you get into your dream school but fail the qualifying exam, then that's not so good.

- What's the process of finding an advisor like? Is it an awkward process, or does the department help to set you up with someone?

- Ask the grad students about the logistics of living in the area. Is it cheaper to live on campus or off? What's the cost of living like? Is a car necessary?

- If you're in particle physics, you'll have to travel to experiments; if you're in nuclear physics, you'll need a nuclear reactor; if you're in astrophysics, you'll need telescopes. Ask about the availability of these facilities, and the travel arrangements. If you're expected to spend months out of the year at another location, you should be paid extra for the cost of maintaining two residences.

- Is there room in my subfield? I have heard heartbreaking stories about brilliant students having to transfer with the program's apologies because there are too few advisors and too many students.

- Ask each professor about the students they have graduated, where they are now, and how long it took them to graduate. There are advisors that haven't had a student graduate in 20 years![1]

- If you get the grad students on their own, ask what their biggest complaints about the program are.

5.2 Negotiations

Negotiations can mean two things: negotiating to be admitted, or negotiating better perks when you are admitted.

Before Admission

Before admission, negotiation is generally only possible if you've been wait-listed. In this case, you may wish to send a letter to one of your prospective advisors explaining the situation. You should summarize your research experience, and directly ask the professor if he/she would consider requesting that you be admitted. You can also e-mail someone on the admissions committee in order to re-express your desire to attend the school, and volunteering to participate in an interview by e-mail or phone.

After Admission

After admission, there's no reason you can't try to get more money (or other perks) out of the program, but you will probably have

---

[1]Though it is possible for advisors to fall into a vicious cycle where they have trouble attracting students, which makes their reputation worse, which gives them more trouble attracting students. So don't be too harsh on professors with few graduated students; just be cautious.

only limited success. One tactic is to give them a copy of your acceptance letter at another school, which offered more money. For this to work, your competing offer should have a similar reputation, facilities, cost of living, and program. Also, the competing offer should be only a little more than your offer – you'll be laughed out of the room if you ask them to double your offer.[2]

You might not have to work so hard. For example, if you are admitted early, it is likely that your letter will say something to the effect of "We haven't decided about fellowships yet. We will contact you if we are able to offer you a fellowship." If you haven't heard anything, you'll often be offered a fellowship simply by asking. But it is often necessary to ask – programs can be hesitant to give fellowship offers to overqualified candidates, because they tend to leave them on the table for months and then decline them. By the time the program is then able to formalize the declination and offer the fellowship to their second-choice candidate, that student has already accepted a fellowship somewhere else.

Your other option for negotiation is to send an e-mail explaining that you will turn down the offer unless your salary is increased to a certain amount. You don't want to do this as a bluff: they'll usually explain that they don't have any more money available, and you'll have no choice but to decline their offer of admission. Still, it might be worth it if, for example, the salary they offer you is not enough to live on.

---

[2]if the competing offer *is* double your current offer, you should spell out what you're hoping to be offered. For example, "Although Oklahoma offered $40,000 per year, I think Texas A&M might be a better fit, and so I would accept your offer if it could be raised to $25,000."

5.3   What Ifs

As your results come in, you might get something unexpected.

What if I'm offered an MS?

You might receive the news that although you haven't been accepted into a particular school's PhD program, you are offered the chance to earn a Master's Degree. To make it even more complicated, they will occasionally mention that after you get your MS, you may be offered a spot in the PhD program at that time.

This is usually a polite rejection. Still, you may want to carefully consider this offer if it is funded and lists specific criteria that, if met, will guarantee you admission to the PhD program. These offers can also be very useful if you don't get in anywhere else.

What if I don't get in anywhere?

Hopefully this wasn't a surprise, and you already developed a backup plan. If you're sure you want to go to grad school, you should take another year as an undergraduate to do additional research, retake classes that didn't go so well the first time, and spend more time on the application process next year. getting a job for a few years is also an option. By this time it's usually April and it's too late to submit additional applications, but you can also try to find schools that are still accepting applications.

What if my best/only offer doesn't come with funding?

If your best offer doesn't have funding, then it's not your best offer. Don't underestimate how difficult it can be to pay off student loans. If your only offer doesn't come with funding, then you have a more difficult decision. Refer back to section 1.4 for more information about funding.

What if I don't hear back from a school?

It's OK to e-mail and ask for a result in April. If they ignore your e-mail, you should assume that you've been rejected.

What does it mean if I'm "provisionally accepted"?

Most acceptances are provisional. This usually means that the physics department has approved your application, but the graduate school has not yet done so. Graduate schools almost always confirm the department's recommendations. If you're still a senior in college, your acceptance might be provisional on your successfully completing college, or on other specifically enumerated criteria.

Very rarely, your acceptance is provisional on something very serious, such as your graduating from college with a particular QPA, or completing a particular college class with a particular grade. This is very rare because most programs want to know for sure who's coming and who isn't by April – but it does happen every now and then.

What if my best offer is from my undergraduate school?

It is true that it's generally better to do your PhD at a different place than you did your undergraduate. This will give you a broader background, a different perspective on the subject, new networking opportunities, and a change of scenery. Still, these drawbacks are only so important – if the best offer you have is from your undergraduate school, then that's just the way it worked out.

What if I'm accepted, but am told that I'll have to change my subfield?

You should be aware that this happens (very rarely). Beyond that, you'll just have to consider your options and make a decision.

What if I'm accepted, but my significant other is not?

As I discussed in section 1.6, this happens fairly regularly for students who are in a relationship. After one of you is admitted, you should tell the department about your relationship, and ask them to review your partner's application. This will usually cause your partner's applications to be reviewed again, more favorably. Recall that offers are made at the convenience of the *program*: so long as your partner is qualified for the program, it may be in the program's best interest to make an offer to him/her (since they'll get two qualified, happy grad students instead of maybe getting one lonely one.)

If your significant other is in a different department, then you can ask your program to put in a word with his/her department – but you will probably have very limited success.

What if I don't like any of the places I got in? Will I be able to transfer after a year or two?

Probably not. Most schools don't accept transfer applications, and acceptance rates for the schools that do accept transfer applications are very low. Beyond that, your work completed at your first graduate school probably won't transfer to the second graduate school.

5.4   Making a Decision

When to make a decision?

You can make your decision as early as you like, though of course it is probably wise to wait until all your acceptances or rejections come in. By agreement of the Council of the Graduate Schools, no program will force you to accept or decline an offer before April 15.

Just because you don't *have* to make a decision before April 15 doesn't mean you shouldn't. You may know early on that you won't be attending one school; you should let that program know immediately that you will not be attending. This is considered common courtesy, and will free up your spot so that another student may be admitted.

Resist the temptation to e-mail your graduate schools in January asking for a decision: such e-mails are annoying and unhelpful, as committees are unlikely to have made any decisions yet. If you still haven't received a decision by April 1, it's OK to send an e-mail asking for your application status – sometimes you're actually still being considered; other times they just haven't gotten around to rejecting you yet.

In rare cases, you will not have received a decision by April 15th, even after asking for one. In this case, you should assume that you've been rejected unless you've received an e-mail telling you that you're still being considered. If you're still being considered, be aware that there's no reason *they* have to make a decision before the 15th; they can accept you weeks after the deadline if they're so inclined.

This is perhaps the stickiest situation: if you commit to somewhere else on the 15th, then you might be giving up the chance to go to your first choice school, should they admit you after the 15th. But if you don't commit to somewhere else on the 15th, then you might not be able to go anywhere. There's no brilliant way out of this dilemma, but my advice is that it's too risky to wait. If it turns out that you are accepted to your reach school, then you can ask the school you committed to for permission to withdraw your acceptance; these are almost always granted (though it's a very awkward situation). In most cases, it's best to withdraw any outstanding applications on the 15th.

Things to consider

Let me repeat what I said in chapter 3:

- Don't go somewhere that will make you miserable – you'll be less productive.

- Don't ignore reputation: if prospective employers don't believe that your degree is meaningful, then it won't matter what research you conducted.

- Make sure you choose a school with a few professors that you would be happy to work for.

A good starting place for making a decision is therefore the following:

1. Rank your offers in terms of their degree quality and reputation – this will probably be a tie.[3] For example, it's common to have a few schools tied for "good quality/reputation" and a few more tied for "lower quality/reputation." As discussed in the rankings section, it's very difficult to draw meaningful distinctions between the quality or reputation of two programs.

2. Mark any schools that seem like they're a less good fit for you.

3. Mark any schools with less than three professors that you'd be happy to work with.[4]

4. Choose the school(s) with the highest "quality/reputation" that you did not mark in steps 2 or 3. If there's more than one school in this category, choose from between those using any criteria you like – money, climate, friends, etc.

You might not want to literally use this algorithm: there are other factors that you may find important. Nonetheless, this is a good

---

[3]Again, degree quality and reputation depends a lot on what your plans are. If you want to be a university professor, the rankings and research opportunities are most important. If you want to get a particular job in a particular city, placement rates and the skills you learn are more important.

[4]Depending on your subfield, you may need to lower this number. For example, you will be hard pressed to find three prospective advisors if your area of interest is acoustic physics.

representation for what your thought process should be. For a more sophistical analysis of your options, I've included a worksheet (see section 7.7) that will allow you to do an objective, side-by-side comparison your offers based on the merits.

Let me finish this section by including a few notes on my algorithm. First, be careful how you define "quality/reputation" in step one. The rankings are only a starting place: there are many factors to consider including placement rates, and the robustness of research in your subfield of interest. The reputation of your advisor is also important; consider the publications and funding statuses of all of your potential advisors.

Second, when comparing salaries, you'll need to adjust your salary for the cost of living. There are many online cost of living calculators – use one of them to determine how much $1 in your prospective city is worth in your current city – that's called the relative index. Take the salary you were offered at each school and divide by that city's relative index – then you can directly compare these "adjusted salaries."

Since your biggest variable costs will be rent and university fees, another option for comparing salaries is to look up how much you'll be paying for rent (easy to find, look on University's housing website if you want to live on campus; Craigslist if not) and how much you'll pay each month to the university in fees (this is often zero, but might be a few hundred bucks). Subtract these expenses from your salary, and you can compare the remaining amounts directly between the schools you are considering (you'll spend the remaining money on food, entertainment, transportation, etc., and those costs are fairly uniform).

A third factor to consider is insurance (*ins.* on the worksheet in section 7.6). Does your program provide health insurance (most do)? Dental (rare)? Optical (rare)? For health insurance, what percentage of costs do they pay (typically 80% or 90%)?

If you find yourself comparing climates, bear in mind that they do the visits in the spring because that's when the campuses are at their most appealing. The Midwest is pretty in the spring, but it's very hot in the summer and very cold in the winter. The South's heat might be a nice change in February, but it's stifling in the summer. California's year round vacation weather might seem perfect when visiting for a few days, but having the same weather day after day for five years can actually be a big adjustment.

You should also consider whether you would be *able* to graduate from the program. How hard are the qualifying exams? How many required courses are there, and how hard are they? How many students fail out each year?[5] If you have trouble taking tests and your prospective school has a week-long qualifying exam, that's something to consider.

---

[5]By the way, don't think you're more likely to fail out just because you were wait-listed. Being wait-listed has less to do with you and more to do with the program's needs for that year.

Accepting & Declining

Accepting an offer is easy – they normally tell you exactly what to do (go to the website and sign the "Statement of Intent to Register" at most schools). Rejecting is equally easy: you should send an e-mail to the graduate secretary and/or the admissions director (both is a more appropriate choice if you visited the campus). Your e-mail could be something like the following:

To whom it may concern:

Thank you for accepting me to your graduate program. I very much enjoyed visiting your campus last month. Unfortunately, I can only attend one school, and I feel that the University of Wisconsin, Madison is a better choice for my particular research goals. As such, please consider this written notice that I must unfortunately decline your offer of admission.

Best wishes,

Vincent Klug

This only gets complicated if something comes up that causes you to change your mind:

- If it's before April 15, then you can withdraw any acceptance of admission you've made.

- Schools are under no obligation to reinstate an offer that you've declined, but they will normally do so if you ask them before April 15.

- If it's after April 15, you'll have to ask for permission to withdraw your acceptance and accept a different offer instead (this is *very* rare, but permission is generally given when it does happen).

- If it's after April 15, it is no problem to withdraw your acceptance if you're not planning to go to grad school at all (all they can do is blacklist you from attending grad school, and that won't matter if you're not going to attend grad school).

Chapter 6

Summer Before Grad School

Now that the application process is over, you have an entire summer to spend before starting grad school.

Some things are non-optional. These include:

- Making plans to relocate, if necessary. If you're moving far, this can be expensive and time consuming, so get started early. If you want to live on campus, there may be a wait list.

- Earning Money. Be aware that you may not get your first check as a graduate student until October or later; long after you go through the very expensive process of relocating, buying textbooks, paying rent (and a security deposit), etc. The good news is you might be able to earn this money while doing research, either for your undergraduate school, graduate school, or a different institution altogether.

- Staying in touch with your graduate program: you may be expected to attend an orientation before the term begins. They may also assign homework over the summer.

- Being aware about entrance exams. Many schools give entrance exams to newly arriving students; your score on this exam may determine whether you need to repeat undergraduate coursework, or if you might be permitted to skip some graduate coursework.

Beyond the requirements, you may be wondering what else you could be doing to improve your graduate experience. There are really three options here: relax, learn useful skills, or prepare for coursework.

Relaxing

Relaxing is a very reasonable option. You've been working hard for four or more years, including the summers probably, and you're about to work hard for five or more additional years. This is a good time to catch up on sleep, pick up your hobbies, learn those new things you've been putting off, and so forth. Even if you don't choose this option, you should pace yourself over the summer; you don't want to burn out.

Studying

Preparing for coursework is maybe a good idea if you're worried about your coursework background. The most difficult of the first year graduate classes is generally electricity & magnetism.

- Electricity & Magnetism: The undergraduate text by David Griffiths is expected background knowledge – if you're not familiar with that book, you should study it over the summer. Jackson's book *Classical Electrodynamics* is almost universally used at the graduate level – but it is *very* hard and *very* dense. A good intermediate text is *Electromagnetic Radiation* by Marion and Heald.

- Classical Mechanics: the most common graduate text is Goldstein's *Classical Mechanics*, but there are other options as well (such as that by Fetter & Wallecka). In any case, you're almost certainly going to start with the calculus of variations, Lagrange's Equations, and Hamilton's Equations.

- Quantum Mechanics: The most common book is definitely Sakurai's *Quantum Mechanics* – it's very accessible. Shankar and Merzbacher both have widely used texts as well. A less commonly used but perhaps more helpful book is written by Cohen-Tannoujidi – his discussion is very thorough.

- Statistical Mechanics: I am not aware of any "standard" book in this course, for undergraduate or graduate. By definition, it's rather difficult to approach this subject systematically, and by the third week, it has usually devolved into doing lots of partial derivatives. Personally, I prefer Huang's book, but everyone has their own preference.

Gathering Skills

In fact, you might not want to get started with graduate coursework right away – time enough for that when the year starts. Instead, you could use the time to develop any research skills that you have not yet picked up. These include:

- A programming language. No matter whether you're working in theory or experiment, you'll have to write in a computer language at some point. Every subfield of physics has its own software, but most these days are based on C++ (or its prequel, FORTRAN, but FORTRAN is old and getting older). If you're thinking of learning a programming language, Python is a good choice: it's easy to learn, powerful, has a nice graphics interface (if you want a graphic simulation, for example), and fast enough for most purposes. It's also a short jump from Python to C++.

- LaTeX. If you've been writing lab reports for the past four years using Microsoft Equation Editor, then you've probably been wondering if there isn't some better way to do it. LaTeXis that way – it's a smarter typesetting language specifically designed for typesetting equations professionally. You'll almost certainly have to use this software to write your dissertation, and probably before that; it's also very easy to learn, and downloads for free from www.ctan.org. For a tutorial, do a Google search for the PDF document entitled "The Not So Short Introduction to LaTeX."

- Mathematical analysis software. By far the most commonly used such software is Mathematica; other options are Maple, MathCad, and Matlab. Of these, Mathematica is probably the most common and most powerful, while MathCad is more user friendly. Check out both your undergraduate and graduate institution, either of them might give you this expensive software for free.

- Unix. Windows is not widely used in physics research. The preferred operating system has traditionally been Linux, but many now prefer Mac – it is more user-friendly in general and has a Terminal application that works almost identically to Linux. If you own a Windows machine, you can set up a dual-boot so that it can run Linux[1]. Linux is free to download, but it does take some getting used to.[2]

---

[1]Though I don't recommend this; I would instead wait until you have an advisor, then ask him/her to provide you with an appropriate computer. My (limited) experience is that Windows computers are noticeably less stable after the operating system is modified.

[2]Better yet, LaTeX is often pre-installed on Linux; installing it on Windows is a bit of a chore.

Chapter 7

Appendices

7.1 Useful References

US News & World Report ranks the physics graduate programs (as discussed in sec. 3.1). These are available online at: http://grad-schools.usnews.rankingsandreviews.com/best-graduate-schools/top-science-schools/physics-rankings.

National Research Council does the other ranking of the physics graduate programs (again, as discussed in sec. 3.1). These are available online at: http://chronicle.com/article/NRC-Rankings-Overview-Physics/124754/. These rankings are a bit hard to read: the ranking is a range of numbers which they call R-high and R-low. You can compare programs by comparing their ranges of scores.[1]

GRE: Practicing to take the General GRE, by ETS. There are many

---

[1] Either or both of these URLs may have changed: a Google search for "US News & World Report Graduate Physics Rankings" or "NRC graduate physics rankings" will find these fairly easily

excellent guides for studying for the general GRE. This one is written by the people who make the test. The downside is that there are no computer tests included. While the paper scores and the computer scores correspond pretty well for most people, it breaks down a bit for those (like you) who are hoping for a near perfect score on the math section. Other options are the books made by Kaplan, Princeton Review, and Barron's (among others) – these do contain computer-based practice tests.

Gradcafe. This is one site that contains forums for admissions-related questions & answers – but this information is not always accurate. A useful (though insanity-inducing) feature of this site is that it allows applicants to submit their results as they come in, so you can monitor which schools have already started making offers. This real time information is at: http://thegradcafe.com/survey/index.php?q=physics&t=a&pp=25.

Writing a Successful College Application Essay, by George Ehren-haft.   This is one of the best of the books I mentioned in section 4.3 about writing an *undergraduate* college admissions essay. It contains specific hints for how to do all parts of the college essay; better yet, it has samples of college admissions essays with specific feedback for each. It will be useful not just for your statement of purpose, but for all essays your programs ask for.

A Review of Undergraduate Physics, by Bayman and Hamermesh. This is exactly as advertised: it provides a good review of everything you should have learned, plus a bit more. The level is a bit too high to be useful for the PGRE, but it's perfect for any other purpose, including studying for many qualifying exams.

Books about the PGRE

There have been three books written about the Physics GRE.[2] One is the one produced by ETS, containing the four practice tests. It's out of print and contains no information that you can't get online. The other two are below.

GRE Physics, by John Molitoris (not recommended). The second is Molitoris's book. Despite the very limited selection, I definitely don't recommend buying Molitoris's book – many students feel that this book actually lowered their scores because the practice tests he provides are inordinately and misleadingly difficult.

Conquering the Physics GRE, by Kahn and Anderson. This is far and away the best book available for GRE prep: written by two MIT students, it provides a detailed review and practice tests. There are a few errors, but the authors maintain a list of errata at their website.[3]

Textbooks at the level of the PGRE

University Physics with Modern Physics, by Freedman and Young. This is my favorite basic physics book. It has both a broad range and depth that corresponds well to the PGRE. The 10th edition in particular is well-written and affordable. Each chapter also has a

---

[2]Not including this one, since the PGRE is only a small part of this book.

[3]Full disclosure: Kahn & Anderson's book came out after I took the exam, so my knowledge of it is purely second-hand.

nice list of questions – the theory questions are particularly good to review. The other ubiquitous textbook is *Fundamentals of Physics by Halliday & Resnick.*

Div, Grad, Curl and all that, by H. M. Schey This is a universally-loved book on vector calculus. Most of these ideas should be familiar to you after completing your E&M sequence, but this is nonetheless a useful review on this topic.

Introduction to Electrodynamics, by David Griffiths. This is just about the only E&M book that's used in undergraduate physics programs. You'll want to be as familiar as possible with chapters 1-3, 5, 7, the easy parts of chapter 9, and section 12.1. If you have time, learn the basic ideas of the remaining chapters. The boxed results in chapter 11 are also good to memorize. Most of the E&M problems on the exam come from the basic physics book, though, so spend the majority of your time with that one.

Introduction to Quantum Mechanics, by David Griffiths. Again, this is just about the only quantum book that you'll need. You should know chapter 1-4 as well as possible. Also know how to find the energy eigenvalues for first order nondegenerate perturbation theory. The other chapters are unlikely to come up at all. If you haven't had undergraduate quantum yet, it's probably not worth studying this unless you have lots of extra time. Only a small number of questions on the PGRE will require this book, so don't get bogged down in it.

Classical Mechanics, by John Taylor. This is my favorite of the undergraduate classical mechanics books. All you really need to know is the behavior of springs (damped and driven), Lagrangians, and Hamiltonians.

I should recommend a book for statistical mechanics, but I really can't bring myself to do so. I hate every text I've ever read on this subject. Moreover, very few if any statistical mechanics questions at this level will appear on the PGRE. The thermo section of your intro book – plus a little knowledge about partition functions – should be sufficient.[4]

---

[4]Chad Orzel wrote a piece for Scienceblogs about this topic, which might be worth a read for at least one perspective on "why stat mech courses suck."

7.2   Cramming for the PGRE

This is in no way designed to be comprehensive – see sec. 2.3 for details on how to comprehensively study for the GRE. Still, if it is the night before and you have yet to open a book, here is a quick checklist.

Part 1: Specific Stuff

This is just a list of quick facts that you should be familiar with. Some of this may be altogether new to you – but none of it's that complicated, and these ideas come up quite regularly.

- Rotational motion: memorize the common formulas for moments of inertia, and understand the parallel axis theorem. Brush up on torque and classical angular momentum.

- Formulas for interference: single slit, double slit, diffraction grating, etc. Where are maxima/minima and what is intensity pattern?

- Radiation: learn basic radioactive decays (alpha, beta, gamma, etc.).

- Diffraction-limited imaging (this is the formula with the 1.22 in it!).

- Memorize the ground state of the hydrogen atom, and (qualitatively) the definition of the Bohr radius. The eigenvalues and eigenvectors for a particle in a box are also good to memorize.

- Learn some constants: especially G, $\hbar$, ϵ_0, and μ_0.

- Filters – which is high pass, which is low pass? Properties of each. Study LC/RC circuits and learn simple properties of each, including time constants.

- Boltzmann Radiation – what emits it? What's the relationship between E and T for a blackbody? What is the "ultraviolet catastrophe"?

- How to read a log-log chart (most questions can be answered by getting three ordered pairs from log-log chart and plotting them on a linear graph).

- Be familiar with basic ideas of photoelectric effect, Rutherford experiment and the Compton effect.

- Types of elementary particles. Be able to classify particles as bosons, fermions, leptons, baryons, etc. Also learn the leptons, quarks, and the vector bosons (there are only a handful of each).

- Difference between Bose-Einstein condensate and Fermi-Dirac Condensate (know the formulas!).

- Be able to take a line, surface, and volume integral in Cartesian, spherical and cylindrical coordinates.

- Complex impedance.

- What is Bremssstrahlung?

- Optical instruments – telescopes and microscopes.

- Method of images.

- Positronium. Every journal article ever written about the PGRE notes the test's apparent fascination with positronium.

- Special relativity. Know the common paradoxes (twin, barn and pole, etc.) and how to do fairly straightforward time dilation/length contraction problems.

- How does a laser work (very basic ideas only?).

- Larmor formula.

- Memorize the equation for wavelengths of hydrogen spectrum.

- Bracket notation.

- Definition (and properties) of an Hermitian operator and of a unitary operator.

- Doppler effect – for sound and for light. Yes, this means memorizing the formulas.

- Lagrangians and Hamiltonians. How to get the equation of motion from each?

- Electron orbital notation: $1s^2$, $2s^2$, etc.

- What are the Stern-Gerlach, Zeeman, and Stark effects?

- Partition functions (if you haven't seen this before, just look at a particle's probability of occupying a given state when there are two options).

- Dielectrics – formulas and concepts.

- L_z in spherical coordinates. This is just about the only way they can test quantum mechanical angular momentum quickly, so it comes up often.

Part 2: Easy Stuff

These are the simple ideas that you've probably forgotten over the years. It would be quite difficult to learn all of this stuff quickly – but fortunately you already know it all; just do examples.

- Gauss's Law and Ampere's Law – do examples!

- Calculating the field from a charge/current distribution.

- Ray tracing diagrams (for lenses and mirrors, concave and convex). Yes, memorize the rules for all four combinations.

- Units for all quantities – be able to get everything (power, impulse, etc.) back to base units.

- Hooke's Law (and general spring behavior).

- Inductance and EMF.

- For kinematic problems, when to use conservation of energy; when to use conservation of momentum?

- How does dispersion work? What is index of refraction? Magnetic Susceptibility? Electric permeability? Dielectric constant? Magnetization?

- Vectors – which way will the vector point for a given type of motion? Practice for velocity, acceleration, force, and field vectors.

- Right hand rule – practice. Only works for positive charges! When is a coordinate system right handed?

Part 3: Further Cramming

If you finish all this and still have a little extra time, I suggest going to the practice exams. Do the practice exams as best you can, and look up anything that you've forgotten. If you find yourself struggling on the optics or thermo questions, you should crack out your intro to physics book and open to those sections. These two subjects together comprise 19% of the exam, and these questions are pretty easy (it's difficult to write a "tricky" thermo or optics question that can be solved in under five minutes). Get through as many of the practice tests as you can, and study your weaknesses. There are 400 practice questions that have been released, but don't go too fast – it's better to remember how to do 100 of them than to have forgotten all 400.

7.3   Rushing the Statement of Purpose

Chapter 4 gives you detailed instructions for writing the statement of purpose, but I am intentionally vague at times so that I do not stifle your creativity. If you have very limited time to write your statement of purpose, then we'll have to risk it. Start by going back to read section 4.3: the specific do's and don'ts there are still very important. Further, I give a series of step-by-step instructions here.

Introduction

This paragraph has three goals: (a) get the committee's attention, (b) introduce yourself to the committee, and (c) explain why you want to do physics. Try to think of a story that would convey your personality to the committee. Another option is to think of some story, philosophy, opinion, or daily practice you do that you could share with the committee. Whatever story you pick should be short, relevant, and recent. Try to phrase this in an interesting or unusual way – you don't want to bore the committee.. You'll then want to segue from your story into a candid discussion of why you want to study physics. If you know what subfield you want to study, you can instead discuss why you want to study that particular subfield.

Research Experience

If you have very little research experience, you may want to reverse the order of this section and the next one.

This section will *discuss* your research experience – I say discuss as opposed to list, your experiences are already listed on your CV.

Instead, discuss what you did as a researcher. What was a typical day like? What skills did you learn? What did you like or dislike about your research? Do you want to stick with the same subfield? What parts of that subfield interest you? What did you like about working with your advisor? What sort of traits do you think your graduate advisor should have? What would you do differently if you had it to do over again? Will these skills and experiences be transferable to grad school? These are just a sampling of the questions you could answer during this section – the point is to discuss what you gained, what you contributed, and how that will help you be a better grad student.

Coursework

Again, this is the section to *discuss* your coursework, not to repeat your CV or your transcript. Instead, mention which courses you found to be the most interesting, or the most challenging. What interesting experiences did you have in your coursework that shaped your research skills? Discuss any non-science coursework that is relevant to your application. A *brief* explanation for poor grades is also acceptable.

Other Experiences

This is where you can explain anything else that aided your development as a potential grad student. This could be a job, volunteer experience, extra-curricular experience, role on a committee, political activism, or anything else. Share how this has impacted you and how it will make you a better grad student.

Conclusion

Conclude that graduate school is a good match for someone with your experiences and your interests, and mention what specific qualities you like about the graduate school you're applying too. You don't want to be too specific here (the program may have changed since its website was last updated). But you should be candid: there is some reason you're applying to this program, what is it?

Revisions

Now that you have a first draft written, you'll want to spend as much time as possible revising it. Use the techniques in section 4.3, but in particular, read the essay over and over again, looking for anything that sounds awkward, wordy, meaningless, or boring. Have the spelling and grammar checked by anyone who's willing to read it.

7.4   Sample Statements of Purpose

Here I present two real essays written by two real students, with commentary. These students seem pretty qualified, so don't be overly alarmed if you have fewer experiences to point to! I have left these uncorrected for spelling and grammar, though I did shorten them a bit (I added ellipses to indicate where I removed details) and change some of the names.

Essay 1

Thanks to Ümit Selahatting Üner for permission to use his essay.

"When I learned how to read and write at the age of 4, I met the joy of learning things. After that, my life has been all about asking questions and learning. When I started to study at the age of 5, two years earlier than normal school age in Turkey, my passion of learning got even bigger. When grow-ups asked me about what I am going to be in future, the one and only answer I gave them was "scientist". I was caught by excellence of science.

After the University Entrance Exam, all of my choices were chemistry or other natural sciences. Then, in the first year of university, I had a chance to get in the modern physics world. I must admit, I was impressed. In next 3 years, while I am studying chemistry, I was trying to keep up with the developments in modern physics. Here I have to say something really bothered me. In my 3rd year, I wanted to improve my skills in modern physics by following lectures in our Physics Department. However, a lecturer, who gives the Introduction to Particle Physics course, did not even let me listen his lessons, and gave me no reason. What would one do in that case? I went home and prepared a presentation. The title was "Particle Physics and Standard Model". The only person I invited from our Physics Department, the one and only member of CERN in our university, said he is totally impressed.

In summer 2008, I had to work as an intern in any field related to chemistry. I choosed the best possible place to work closely with Nuclear Sciences, Cekmece Nuclear Research and Training Center. After my obligated one month work, [my advisor] there requested me to stay another month to work with him. Of course, I eagerly accepted this request. Besides, in that summer I attended to 4th National Summer School on Particle Accelerators and Detectors in Turkey, organised by Turkish Physical Society and that's where I met the Synchrotron Radiaton....It was the event which introduced me to MAX-Lab.

MAX-Lab, the only laboratory of its kind in Sweden, looked as a very amazing place to study - or work - for me, because I have been to Sweden twice before and I was already impressed by the people living here. Their respect to each other, their respect to nature was showing that the people here are living in a great harmony. Also I must say I have a belief that studying at MAX-Lab as a Master's Degree student would be a unique opportunity to enrich my knowledge in the fields of my interests and to continue the career path I have started in an academic environment and I intend to follow this up with a Ph.D.

In Fall Semester 2008, I was an instructor in the laboratory of Nuclear Chemistry I course. My thesis advisor Prof. U. had troubles with finding Ph.D. students with enough experience in Nuclear Chemistry, then I came up with an idea, I said I could do it....As the course ended last week, students kept telling me they really like my experiments....Nowadays, we are working intensively on our diploma....My specialized subject is about coding a computer software which can calculate the behaviors of F-18 radioactive isotope in a cell using Monte Carlo calculations and its consequences. Other research areas of us includes new aspects in PET imaging, using F-18 isotope with novel studies and so on.

Since we don't have any particle accelerators for research, studying in the field of Synchrotron Radiation Based Sciences is nearly impossible in Turkey. MAX-Lab gives me the opportunity for studying in a cutting-edge research field. Including Sweden's countless chances for scientists working there....I remember Alfred B. Nobel once wrote in a letter as an answer to a question asking where he lives; "Home is where I work, and I work everywhere". Taking all these benefits of Sweden and my addiction to science into account, I eagerly want to study in MAX-Lab und jag önskar innerligt att Sverige skall bli mitt nya hem."

The good:

- There are some good details that I wouldn't have known otherwise: his invitation to stay on in Cekmece, his prior knowledge about Sweden/Swedish, and his intention to seek a PhD.

- He makes a convincing case that MAX-Lab is a logical choice for him; I don't get the impression that he's just applying everywhere.

- He makes a good point that Turkey has limited research opportunities (which we may not have realized), without the impression of making excuses.

- The author seems to genuinely enjoy his career; further, he seems to take the initiative in seeking out opportunities.

The bad:

- The first paragraph should be totally changed. It is boring, provides no real information, and the author seems to take bizarre pride having learned to read at the age of four.

- The second paragraph too is a bit bizarre. While I can understand his frustration at being excluded from the lectures, I question his decision to complain about this in his statement of purpose. It's also not clear why his presentation about the standard model was a logical or effective response to this exclusion. (This is a great detail to include, but it should be motivated a bit differently.)

- I'd like to learn a bit more about the research. The details presented here give a general overview, but I'd want to know more about exactly what was done and how the author specifically contributed.

- Each paragraph should have one topic. For example, the penultimate paragraph seems to talk about his teaching experience, but then it ends by talking about his research. I would rather see more specific details about each in two different paragraphs. The last paragraph has similar issues.

- There are a few spelling and grammar mistakes: "the Synchrotron Radiaton", and "research areas of us includes", for example.

- There are several vague statements about how this is "a unique opportunity to enrich my knowledge" (and some stereotypical, though flattering, statements about Swedes).

- Finally, the author comes across as a bit arrogant. To some extent that is inevitable in a paper like this one, but there are things that can be done to minimize this. For example, the author writes, "The only person I invited from our Physics Department, the one and only member of CERN in our university, said he is totally impressed". This could be rephrased, for example: "This talk was well-received; in particular, I was honored to receive positive feedback from the CERN member based at our University."

Essay 2

Thanks to Andrew Ulvestad for permission to use his essay.

"Dry ice, water, and a plastic soda bottle made a pretty impressive explosion, at least to a thirteen year old. However, I was always drawn to theory because it is an essential predictive tool, an absolutely necessary prerequisite to experiment and the idea that equations on a piece of paper can describe physical situations always was, and is, fascinating. Not to mention my last experiment, on the optimum mixture of dry ice and water, exploded in my thirteen year old hand.

It was hour 9, cherry coke number two and I was on the hunt to understand why this cross term had magically vanished. Papers, books, google books, and many a Wikipedia article later, it all finally clicked and I was temporarily satisfied to end the journey. This was a typical day in summer 2008, which I spent investigating the linear stability of an idealized planetary core with Stefan, a professor in our department. I reproduced the theoretical and numerical results, with my own independent code, of a previous paper concerned with the Stokes boundary layer formed by an oscillating flat plate....

Though my interests have ultimately strayed from fluid dynamics, my experience with Stefan was formative....I was given a lot of independence and thus was forced to learn how to make decisions on my own, ask the right questions, and learn how to find the answers given my available resources, which did not often include simply asking Stefan. Most importantly, I emerged with confidence in my own research ability and the conviction that theoretical research was the correct path to pursue in my life.

My initial interest in plasma physics stemmed from a sophomore course on energy systems that had the students explicitly calculated quantities of each competing alternative energy source necessary to replace oil and coal. The disparity of scales, 1 kg of deuterium vs. 100 square miles of wind farms, left an impression. I learned that the confinement problem was essentially a turbulence problem, but work with Stefan and school put magnetic fusion on the back burner. In the fall, however, the stars aligned and I landed in the graduate plasma physics course....

Hundreds of emails and many late nights later, I gradually began formulating a system that, ideally, would permit the investigation of previously unexplored flow regimes. In contrast to previous works, our model did not rely on weak coupling or perturbative methods.... Our results suggest a possible reconciliation between long standing, seemingly contradictory, observations of fast pulse propagation and bulk Gryo-Bohm confinement scaling in tokamaks.... What I have done is only a beginning, but the techniques I learned, most importantly the art of getting unstuck, and my conviction that further research is the only path to take are applicable and necessary to success in any area of research.

I want to pursue more theoretical research in graduate school and there is, arguably, no better place to do this than M.I.T. First and foremost, M.I.T. is host to PSFC which is clearly dedicated to being a leader in fusion confinement. Specifically, Dr. X's recent work on controlling edge plasma rotation is directly linked to my work on zonal flow and transport barrier formation. Similarly, Dr. Y's work on the accretion theory of spontaneous rotation in toroidal plasma is also relevant....Plasma physics is clearly a very active area of research at M.I.T. and there are multiple professors that would challenge and push me to the highest possible level of research. I will also be able to broaden my general knowledge of physics by learning from people who did the fundamental work in diverse subjects, including general relativity and quantum field theory.

From a logistical standpoint, the Physics department is committed to minimizing distractions and maximizing research. I like that the department....makes it straight forward to investigate other research groups and facilitates transfers between groups by guaranteeing funding. There is also unrivaled community support specifically for physics graduate students in the form of Resources for Easing Friction and Stress, or REFS.... In short, M.I.T. is an ideal place to make fundamental contributions to the field of plasma physics because of the outstanding research being done by the faculty and the impressive departmental commitment to minimizing the problems and worries of graduate life while maximizing research and research opportunities.

M.I.T. is also appealing from a personal point of view. I went to high school in Rhode Island and have many close friends that go to school in Boston and the surrounding areas. I am also very close with my family, which still lives about ten minutes south of Providence."

The Good

- Excellent discussion of research. I have a sense for what he did, not only overall, but also on a day-to-day basis. I understand his interests and accomplishments, and have a mental picture of him as a problem solver.

- Good discussion of the reasons for his application: in addition to the obvious reasons (it's MIT), he gives very several specific reasons why he should attend.

- The first paragraph is pretty good; it tells me that he is committed to theory and gives a slightly humorous anecdote about the experiment exploding.

- I really like the detail he included about 1 kg of deuterium vs. 100 square miles of wind farms. Remember the professors reviewing your application are physicists, and will be as fascinated by that fact as you are.

- Good discussion of strengths without sounding arrogant – "what I have done is only a beginning" is a great phrase to make yourself more likeable.

- Listing professors is a good thing to do. Further, Andrew does a good job of being very general, since he has presumably not discussed his plans with these professors.[5]

The Bad

- The last paragraph should be removed or rewritten. It is good to talk about something other than research, but these details are not very interesting. Further, it does not make sense to put these details as the conclusion of the essay.

- The writing in places is a little pedestrian (for example, "This was a typical day....") Further, the capitalization in a few

---

[5] It's quite likely that one of the professors you mention will read your application, so you don't want to say that you plan to work with him/her on a very specific project (since you'll be screwed if the professor turns out to be uninterested in your project). On the other hand, if you have spoken to the professor, it's a good idea to mention this.

places is off, and the word "tokamak" is undefined. The evaluators are physicists, so it's fine to talk about turbulence, perturbation theory, etc. – but I think "tokamak" is a bridge too far.

- The paper is a little long – I cut it down a bit for this book, but it was originally over 1000 words long (some schools ask for 500, others give you 700-800).

7.5   Sample CV

This is a *sample* CV for a highly-qualified student. Don't be alarmed if your CV is significantly different; in particular, yours might be much longer or shorter.

VINCENT L. KLUG

Department of Physics	4500 Main Street, Burlington, VT, 05401
University of Vermont	VK@vermont.edu ◊ (603) 555-0174

Objective

To obtain a position as a graduate student so that I can conduct original research in condensed matter physics while earning my PhD. I hope to use this training as a research physicist for the nanofabrication industry.

Education

B.S., University of Vermont, 2012

- Major in physics with honors, and mathematics

- Minor in theatre arts

- QPA of 3.89, including 10 courses through the honors college.

- GRE: 650 (verbal), 800 (math), 5.5 (writing)

- Physics GRE: 820

Research Experience

Student Researcher, University of Vermont, 2009-2012

- Conducted original research in experimental condensed matter physics, under the guidance of Dr. Alan Smith

- Investigated the scattering pattern of nanosecond pulses from a Helium-Argon laser on a graphene target

- Participated in data taking, laser construction, sample preparation, and data analysis using MATLAB

UROP Fellow, University of Illinois, Summer 2009

- Collected original data on extrasolar planets using a telescope during a ten-week summer program at the University of New Hampshire, under the guidance of Dr. Greg Breckman

- Results published by Dr. Breckman in 2011

Teaching Experience

TA, University of Vermont, 2011-2012

- Taught a weekly recitation section of 30 students for physics I; also graded homework

- Received 95% positive student feedback on course evaluations

Skills

- Fluent Spanish

- Proficiency with Mathematica, Matlab, and C++

- Experience with tunneling electron microscope, telescopes, laser design, and preparation of graphene layers

7.6 List of Subfields

I listed in chapter 4 the most common subfields. These are astrophysics, biophysics, condensed matter physics, and elementary particle physics (which is also called high energy physics). Here I will list the other common subfields:

- Acoustics. The study of sound, in particular producing higher quality sound.

- Applied Physics. A application of physics to anything else. Many universities have separate "applied physics" departments; still others do this through the engineering department rather than the physics department.

- Atomic, Molecular, and Optical (AMO) Physics. This is distinct from condensed matter physics (which generally studies larger systems), but the two terms are often used interchangeably.

- Geophysics. The study of the physics of planets.

- Heavy Ion Physics. This is half way between nuclear physics and particle physics; the study of how the particles in a heavy ion interact.

- Mathematical Physics. The application of Mathematics to problems in physics. This is a very small subfield; most of this research is done through the math department (either do a math PhD directly, or else do a physics degree, but your advisor will be a research mathematician).

- Medical Physics. The application of physics to medicine; such physicists are often employed at hospitals or developing new medical equipment.

- Nanophysics: the study of the very small. This is often studied as condensed matter or AMO physics.

- Nuclear Physics. The study of the nucleus: this can refer to exploring the nature of the nucleus, to building new isotopes, or to the engineering of nuclear power.

- Optics/Photonics. Optics is the study of light, often focusing on methods of producing light (lasers) and distributing light (optical fibers). Photonics is the technology of retooling electronics to use photons rather than electrons.

- Physics Education. The study of teaching physics.

- Plasma Physics. The study of plasma: electrically charged gases.

- Quantum Computing. The study of trying to build a quantum computer.

- Solid State Physics. This is distinct from Condensed Matter Physics (which studies non-solid systems as well), but the two are often used interchangeably.

7.7   Worksheets

This section provides three worksheets for you.

1. **Budget Worksheet.** Applying to graduate school is expensive! This worksheet will help you estimate your expenses before filling out the first application.

2. **Application Checklist.** It's easy to forget pieces of applications. This checklist will allow you to keep track of annoying facts (such as logins, passwords, and addresses) and check off application components as you complete them.

3. **Decision Worksheet.** This is one customizable table that will help you compare your offers of admission.

Another helpful hint is to bookmark the useful webpages in your web browser. If you switch computers regularly, try e-mailing the URLs to yourself, or using a service such as Dropbox or Evernote.

Budget Worksheet

Test Costs

GRE General Test: $_____

As of 2011, this test costs $195 worldwide

GRE Subject Test: $_____

As of 2014, this test costs $150 worldwide

Test Fees

Score Reports $_____

*Some schools will accept unofficial GRE
and PGRE scores until you are admitted,
and some do not require GRE scores at
all – though you should still send them if
they are good. You get four score reports
for free, additional ones cost $27 each
(as of 2014).*

Application Fees

Application fees range from free to $100.
or so. As a rule of thumb, you can
guess $70 for first and second tier schools
and $40 for other schools - but you'll want
to look them up as early as possible.

Program Name	Fee
1. _____	$_____
2. _____	$_____
3. _____	$_____
4. _____	$_____
5. _____	$_____
6. _____	$_____
7. _____	$_____
8. _____	$_____
9. _____	$_____
10. _____	$_____
11. _____	$_____
12. _____	$_____
13. _____	$_____
14. _____	$_____
15. _____	$_____

Total: $ _____

Application Checklist

Graduate Program: *University of Alabama, Tuscaloosa*

Username: *VincentKlug100*   Password: *MyPassword*

Addresses: *The Univ. of Alabama*   *Grad. App. Comm.*

           Graduate School   *Physics Dept.*

           PO Box 870118   *PO Box 870324*

           Tuscaloosa, AL, 35487   *Tuscaloosa, AL, 35487*

E-mail: *physgrad@ua.edu*

Letters of Recommendation: ☐   ☐   ☐   ☐

Statement of Purpose: ☐   Transcript(s):   ☐   ☐

GRE Scores: ☐   PGRE Scores: ☐   App Form: ☐

App Fee: ☐   CV: ☐

Graduate Program: _____

Username: _____   Password: _____

Addresses: _____   _____

           _____   _____

           _____   _____

           _____   _____

E-mail: _____

Letters of Recommendation: ☐   ☐   ☐   ☐

Statement of Purpose: ☐   Transcript(s):   ☐   ☐

GRE Scores: ☐   PGRE Scores: ☐   App Form: ☐

App Fee: ☐   CV: ☐

Cross out any boxes you don't need, and write in any additional application components below:

Graduate Program: _____

Username: _____   Password: _____

Addresses: _____   _____

_____   _____

_____   _____

_____   _____

E-mail: _____

Letters of Recommendation: ☐   ☐   ☐   ☐

Statement of Purpose: ☐   Transcript(s): ☐   ☐

GRE Scores: ☐   PGRE Scores: ☐   App Form: ☐

App Fee: ☐   CV: ☐

Cross out any boxes you don't need, and write in any additional application components below:

Graduate Program: _____

Username: _____   Password: _____

Addresses: _____   _____

_____   _____

_____   _____

_____   _____

E-mail: _____

Letters of Recommendation: ☐   ☐   ☐   ☐

Statement of Purpose: ☐   Transcript(s): ☐   ☐

GRE Scores: ☐   PGRE Scores: ☐   App Form: ☐

App Fee: ☐   CV: ☐

Cross out any boxes you don't need, and write in any additional application components below:

Graduate Program: _____

Username: _____   Password: _____

Addresses: _____   _____

              _____   _____

              _____   _____

              _____   _____

E-mail: _____

Letters of Recommendation: □   □   □   □

Statement of Purpose: □   Transcript(s): □   □

GRE Scores: □   PGRE Scores: □   App Form: □

App Fee: □   CV: □

Cross out any boxes you don't need, and write in any additional application components below:

Graduate Program: _____

Username: _____   Password: _____

Addresses: _____   _____

              _____   _____

              _____   _____

              _____   _____

E-mail: _____

Letters of Recommendation: □   □   □   □

Statement of Purpose: □   Transcript(s): □   □

GRE Scores: □   PGRE Scores: □   App Form: □

App Fee: □   CV: □

Cross out any boxes you don't need, and write in any additional application components below:

Graduate Program: _____

Username: _____   Password: _____

Addresses: _____   _____

_____   _____

_____   _____

_____   _____

E-mail: _____

Letters of Recommendation: ☐   ☐   ☐   ☐

Statement of Purpose: ☐   Transcript(s): ☐   ☐

GRE Scores: ☐   PGRE Scores: ☐   App Form: ☐

App Fee: ☐   CV: ☐

Cross out any boxes you don't need, and write in any additional application components below:

Graduate Program: _____

Username: _____   Password: _____

Addresses: _____   _____

_____   _____

_____   _____

_____   _____

E-mail: _____

Letters of Recommendation: ☐   ☐   ☐   ☐

Statement of Purpose: ☐   Transcript(s): ☐   ☐

GRE Scores: ☐   PGRE Scores: ☐   App Form: ☐

App Fee: ☐   CV: ☐

Cross out any boxes you don't need, and write in any additional application components below:

Graduate Program: _____

Username: _____   Password: _____

Addresses: _____   _____

                _____   _____

                _____   _____

                _____   _____

E-mail: _____

Letters of Recommendation: ☐   ☐   ☐   ☐

Statement of Purpose: ☐   Transcript(s): ☐   ☐

GRE Scores: ☐   PGRE Scores: ☐   App Form: ☐

App Fee: ☐   CV: ☐

Cross out any boxes you don't need, and write in any additional application components below:

Graduate Program: _____

Username: _____   Password: _____

Addresses: _____   _____

                _____   _____

                _____   _____

                _____   _____

E-mail: _____

Letters of Recommendation: ☐   ☐   ☐   ☐

Statement of Purpose: ☐   Transcript(s): ☐   ☐

GRE Scores: ☐   PGRE Scores: ☐   App Form: ☐

App Fee: ☐   CV: ☐

Cross out any boxes you don't need, and write in any additional application components below:

Graduate Program: _____

Username: _____   Password: _____

Addresses: _____   _____

           _____   _____

           _____   _____

           _____   _____

E-mail: _____

Letters of Recommendation: ☐ ☐ ☐ ☐

Statement of Purpose: ☐   Transcript(s): ☐   ☐

GRE Scores: ☐   PGRE Scores: ☐   App Form: ☐

App Fee: ☐   CV: ☐

Cross out any boxes you don't need, and write in any additional application components below:

Graduate Program: _____

Username: _____   Password: _____

Addresses: _____   _____

           _____   _____

           _____   _____

           _____   _____

E-mail: _____

Letters of Recommendation: ☐ ☐ ☐ ☐

Statement of Purpose: ☐   Transcript(s): ☐   ☐

GRE Scores: ☐   PGRE Scores: ☐   App Form: ☐

App Fee: ☐   CV: ☐

Cross out any boxes you don't need, and write in any additional application components below:

Graduate Program: _____

Username: _____   Password: _____

Addresses: _____   _____

              _____   _____

              _____   _____

              _____   _____

E-mail: _____

Letters of Recommendation: ☐   ☐   ☐   ☐

Statement of Purpose: ☐   Transcript(s):   ☐   ☐

GRE Scores: ☐   PGRE Scores: ☐   App Form: ☐

App Fee: ☐   CV: ☐

Cross out any boxes you don't need, and write in any additional application components below:

Graduate Program: _____

Username: _____   Password: _____

Addresses: _____   _____

              _____   _____

              _____   _____

              _____   _____

E-mail: _____

Letters of Recommendation: ☐   ☐   ☐   ☐

Statement of Purpose: ☐   Transcript(s):   ☐   ☐

GRE Scores: ☐   PGRE Scores: ☐   App Form: ☐

App Fee: ☐   CV: ☐

Cross out any boxes you don't need, and write in any additional application components below:

Graduate Program: _____

Username: _____   Password: _____

Addresses: _____   _____

_____   _____

_____   _____

_____   _____

E-mail: _____

Letters of Recommendation: ☐   ☐   ☐   ☐

Statement of Purpose: ☐   Transcript(s): ☐   ☐

GRE Scores: ☐   PGRE Scores: ☐   App Form: ☐

App Fee: ☐   CV: ☐

Cross out any boxes you don't need, and write in any additional application components below:

Graduate Program: _____

Username: _____   Password: _____

Addresses: _____   _____

_____   _____

_____   _____

_____   _____

E-mail: _____

Letters of Recommendation: ☐   ☐   ☐   ☐

Statement of Purpose: ☐   Transcript(s): ☐   ☐

GRE Scores: ☐   PGRE Scores: ☐   App Form: ☐

App Fee: ☐   CV: ☐

Cross out any boxes you don't need, and write in any additional application components below:

Graduate Program: _____

Username: _____   Password: _____

Addresses: _____   _____

_____   _____

_____   _____

_____   _____

E-mail: _____

Letters of Recommendation: ☐   ☐   ☐   ☐

Statement of Purpose: ☐   Transcript(s): ☐   ☐

GRE Scores: ☐   PGRE Scores: ☐   App Form: ☐

App Fee: ☐   CV: ☐

Cross out any boxes you don't need, and write in any additional application components below:

Graduate Program: _____

Username: _____   Password: _____

Addresses: _____   _____

_____   _____

_____   _____

_____   _____

E-mail: _____

Letters of Recommendation: ☐   ☐   ☐   ☐

Statement of Purpose: ☐   Transcript(s): ☐   ☐

GRE Scores: ☐   PGRE Scores: ☐   App Form: ☐

App Fee: ☐   CV: ☐

Cross out any boxes you don't need, and write in any additional application components below:

Graduate Program: _____

Username: _____   Password: _____

Addresses: _____   _____

                  _____   _____

                  _____   _____

                  _____   _____

E-mail: _____

Letters of Recommendation: ☐   ☐   ☐   ☐

Statement of Purpose: ☐   Transcript(s): ☐   ☐

GRE Scores: ☐   PGRE Scores: ☐   App Form: ☐

App Fee: ☐   CV: ☐

Cross out any boxes you don't need, and write in any additional application components below:

Graduate Program: _____

Username: _____   Password: _____

Addresses: _____   _____

                  _____   _____

                  _____   _____

                  _____   _____

E-mail: _____

Letters of Recommendation: ☐   ☐   ☐   ☐

Statement of Purpose: ☐   Transcript(s): ☐   ☐

GRE Scores: ☐   PGRE Scores: ☐   App Form: ☐

App Fee: ☐   CV: ☐

Cross out any boxes you don't need, and write in any additional application components below:

Decision Worksheet

Name	Rank	Type of Support	Salary	Rel. Index	Ins.	# Profs			Notes
Example	*75*	*TAship*	*$21,000*	*1.2*	*Yes*	*7*			

Decision Worksheet

Name	Rank	Type of Support	Salary	Rel. Index	Ins.	# Profs			Notes

Final Comments

You may have noticed that I didn't cite a single source in this entire book. To some extent that's because there aren't any: as far as I know, there has never been a book written on physics graduate school admission. So where did this information come from? I've had to attend many lectures on the subject, talk to dozens of professors involved with the application process, and spend hours and hours with various sources, trying to understand this admission process.

I am aware that things vary from school to school, so my judgment should not replace your own. There is a real trade-off between being specific and being accurate – I have tried to be very specific (since general advice is obvious and unhelpful), but you must promise not to assume that the specifics I gave are absolutely and universally true. Similarly, I am not responsible if any of the information in the book negatively affects your application. All I can do here is state how it usually works at most schools, to the best of my knowledge.

Now that you've finished my book, you know as much about the process as I do – but if you need a second opinion, please feel free to e-mail me (vincentklug100@gmail.com); I normally respond within a week. Further, please be sure to e-mail me if:

- you have any comments, questions, or suggestions for the book.

- you are willing to have your statement of purpose printed in the book, with comments (even terrible statements of purpose are useful, and I'll keep it anonymous unless you request otherwise).

- you are highly knowledgeable about the admission process and have feedback

I may write a third edition of this book or hire someone to do so.[6] Your feedback and sample essays would be helpful for those revisions.

Let me end by looking to the future: I hope you will be disappointed at the news that I have no intention of writing a sequel. There are already many excellent books on the topic of getting through grad school: one (very) light-hearted one is *Surviving your stupid stupid decision to go to grad school* by Adam Ruben; several more serious ones are also out there. After you get your PhD, an excellent reference is written by Peter Feibelman, it's called *A PhD is not enough! A guide to survival in Science.*

---

[6]Though at this moment I have no plans to do so. If 2014 was a long time ago and no third edition exists, an update may be called for. Please e-mail me if you are interested in being involved with this (assuming we still use e-mail in the future).

Advertisement

A few applicants have asked about hiring me to help them draft and revise their statements of purpose.[7] This is a possibility: if you are interested, please send me an e-mail (VincentKlug100@gmail.com).

We can discuss rates for your particular needs, but in the past, the following arrangement has worked well: for a set fee, the applicant can get unlimited help for a certain period of time on a particular essay or essays. All e-mails and requests for editing will be answered within 24 hours, and often much faster. The price for this depends on the specifics, but is usually in the range of $150.

If you're wondering whether this is worth it, I would suggest sending me an e-mail and we can have a "free consultation." I recognize that applicants have limited funds, and I will be honest if your essay is already in fine shape. But the truth is that most statements of purpose have a lot of room for improvement; for such applicants, my fee is well worth the money.

---

[7]As mentioned many times, I am willing and eager to answer questions and give general advice by e-mail for free. Here I refer only to students who would like me to spend hours giving line-by-line reviews of their essays

Index